LIBERTARIANISM WITHOUT INEQUALITY

LIBERTARIANISM
WITHOUT
INEQUALITY

MICHAEL OTSUKA

CLARENDON PRESS · OXFORD

OXFORD
UNIVERSITY PRESS

Great Clarendon Street, Oxford OX2 6DP

Oxford University Press is a department of the University of Oxford.
It furthers the University's objective of excellence in research, scholarship,
and education by publishing worldwide in

Oxford New York

Auckland Bangkok Buenos Aires Cape Town Chennai
Dar es Salaam Delhi Hong Kong Istanbul Karachi Kolkata
Kuala Lumpur Madrid Melbourne Mexico City Mumbai Nairobi
São Paulo Shanghai Taipei Tokyo Toronto

Oxford is a registered trade mark of Oxford University Press
in the UK and in certain other countries

Published in the United States
by Oxford University Press Inc., New York

© Michael Otsuka 2003

The moral rights of the author have been asserted
Database right Oxford University Press (maker)

First published 2003

British Library Cataloguing in Publication Data
Data available

Library of Congress Cataloging in Publication Data
Data available

ISBN 0–19–924395–6

1 3 5 7 9 10 8 6 4 2

Typeset by Hope Services (Abingdon) Ltd
Printed in Great Britain
on acid-free paper by
T. J. International Ltd.,
Padstow, Cornwall

For Jerry:
teacher, mentor, comrade, friend

ACKNOWLEDGEMENTS

Chapter 1 is a substantially revised and expanded version of the following article: Michael Otsuka, 'Self-Ownership and Equality: A Lockean Reconciliation', *Philosophy and Public Affairs*, 27/1 (winter 1998): 65–92. Copyright 1998, and reprinted in revised form with permission of, Princeton University Press. The version published here differs from the original article in the following respects: The main thesis regarding the reconciliation of self-ownership and equality, as stated in the introductory remarks and in Section IV, has been reformulated. In Section III I offer a revised formulation and an expanded defence and elaboration of the egalitarian version of the Lockean proviso. In Section V I now offer a proviso-based argument against bequests and argue for the compatibility of self-ownership with the strict egalitarian regulation of the non-market transfer and sharing of resources among members of the same generation. The other sections have been revised to only a minor degree.

Chapter 2 is a revised version of the following article: Michael Otsuka, 'Making the Unjust Provide for the Least Well Off', *Journal of Ethics*, 2/3 (1998): 247–59. Copyright 1998, and reprinted with kind permission of, Kluwer Academic Publishers.

Chapter 3 Section II draws on material originally published in the following article: Michael Otsuka, 'Quinn on Punishment and Using Persons as Means', *Law and Philosophy*, 15/2 (1996): 201–8. Copyright 1996, and reprinted with kind permission of, Kluwer Academic Publishers.

Chapter 4 is a very slightly revised version of the following article: Michael Otsuka, 'Killing the Innocent in Self-Defense', *Philosophy and Public Affairs*, 23/1 (winter 1994): 74–94. Copyright 1994, and reprinted with permission of, Princeton University Press.

Chapters 5–7 consist entirely of previously unpublished material.

In addition to those whom I thank in the originally published versions of the above articles, I would like to acknowledge the following debts: Revised versions of Chapter 1 were presented at King's College, Cambridge, and Yale University. Versions of Chapters 5–6 were presented at the Law and Philosophy Discussion Group in Los Angeles, the University of Exeter, University College London, the University of Liverpool, the London Political Theory Workshop, All Souls College, Oxford, the University of Sheffield, the Universidad Torcuato Di Tella, and the University of Michigan, Ann Arbor. Versions of Chapter 7 were presented at University College London, the University of Bristol, All Souls College, Oxford, the University of Manchester, the London School of Economics, New York University, the University of Warwick, the University of Wisconsin-Madison, and Oberlin College. I thank those who provided helpful comments on these occasions. I would also like to thank John Roemer for his generous written commentary on a revised version of Chapter 1; Alan Carter, John Davidson, Cécile Fabre, Alon Harel, Barbara Herman, Eduardo Rivera López, Véronique Munoz-Dardé, Glen Shadbolt, Seana Shiffrin, Andrew Williams, and Jonathan Wolff for their written comments on versions of Chapters 5–6; John Davidson, Ronald Dworkin, Cécile Fabre, and Alon Harel for their written comments on versions of Chapter 7; and A. John Simmons and Peter Vallentyne for their comments on the manuscript as a whole. In the Spring Term of 2002 I presented Chapters 1 and 5–6 in a seminar at University College London. I would like to thank the participants in this seminar: Miriam Cohen-Christofidis, Brian Feltham, Ben Joicey, Véronique Munoz-Dardé, Thomas Porter, Alex Voorhoeve, and Jonathan Wolff. I am indebted to Brian Feltham for creating the index and Ross Ford for reviewing the page proofs. I thank the Arts and Humanities Research Board for providing me with extended leave during the 2001/2 academic year in order to complete this book, and Peter Momtchiloff at Oxford University Press for being such an encouraging and accommodating editor. I am especially grateful to G. A. Cohen for setting me down the path to this book sixteen years ago, for his guidance along the way, and for his characteristically brilliant and incisive commentary on the penultimate draft.

London   M. O.
February 2003

CONTENTS

Introduction

In the following chapters I will present and defend an approach to political philosophy, and a set of moral and political principles, that draw their inspiration from John Locke's *Second Treatise of Government*.[1] I will develop—and modify and revise as necessary—those ideas in the *Second Treatise* that I find true, interesting, and illuminating of topics of contemporary concern among analytic political philosophers. In so doing, I will cover the main topics of this treatise: one's rights of control over oneself and the world (i.e. one's rights of self- and world-ownership), one's rights to use force in order to defend these rights, and the source and limits of political authority. I would like to end up with more than a ragbag of reflections on various topics each of which has a pedigree that can be traced to some passage or other in Locke, but none of which connects with the reflections on the other topics. Rather, I would like to retrieve an entire system of political thought from the treatise. I believe that Locke managed to apprehend some important truths of political morality, truths that together constitute an elegant and unified system of ideas. He was not, however, always able to apprehend these truths clearly. Even when he was able to grasp these truths, he often did so only in their bare outline or essence. Often he did not fully understand how they were true in detail nor why they were true. His *Second Treatise* was, after all, a pioneering work in developing a systematic and classically liberal political philosophy that derived the legitimate authority of government from the consent of individuals who were regarded as free and equal. Standing on Locke's shoulders, unblinded by the ideology and prejudice of his day, and with the aid of three hundred more years of political thought, I hope, from this superior vantage-point, better to

---

[1] Locke, *Two Treatises of Government*, ed. Peter Laslett (Cambridge: Cambridge University Press, 1988), bk. II.

apprehend and more accurately to represent the system of truths of political morality that Locke first sketched in his *Second Treatise*. In doing so, I aspire to be faithful not to the letter of his text, but to the truths that he sought to represent.

The ideas of the *Second Treatise* have not yet, in my opinion, been fully cleansed of the regressive ideological commitments of Locke's (and more recent) times. His classical liberalism has, in the not-too-distant past, provided an inspiration for the right-wing libertarian political philosophy of Robert Nozick, as spelled out in his book *Anarchy, State, and Utopia*.[2] Even many of Locke's more moderate or left-leaning interpreters have not yet provided a sufficiently egalitarian reconstruction of his political philosophy.[3] I would like to contribute to recent efforts to reclaim Locke from the libertarian right and to show how his writings can provide an inspiration for a strongly egalitarian version of libertarianism. This book might be regarded as an attempt to vindicate, in a more comprehensively systematic fashion than has previously been attempted, a political philosophy that has come to be known as left-libertarianism.[4]

Like all other versions of Lockean libertarianism, mine regards a right of self-ownership as fundamental, where such a right consists of robust and stringent rights of control over oneself: one's mind, body, and life. Such a commitment to self-ownership is, I think, definitive of Lockean libertarianism. The anti-paternalistic and anti-moralistic implications of this right will be attractive to anyone who finds himself in sympathy with the conclusions which John Stuart Mill draws in *On Liberty*.[5] When it comes to such things as freedom of expression, the legalization of euthanasia, of sexual relations of any sort between consenting adults, of the possession of cannabis and other recreational drugs, of gambling, and the like, I am completely at one with other

---

[2] Robert Nozick, *Anarchy, State, and Utopia* (New York: Basic Books, 1974).

[3] Three whom I have in mind are A. John Simmons, *The Lockean Theory of Rights* (Princeton, NJ: Princeton University Press, 1992) and *On the Edge of Anarchy* (Princeton, NJ: Princeton University Press, 1993); Gopal Sreenivasan, *The Limits of Lockean Rights in Private Property* (New York: Oxford University Press, 1995); and David Lloyd Thomas, *Locke on Government* (London: Routledge, 1995).

[4] Hillel Steiner, Peter Vallentyne, and Philippe van Parijs are three prominent proponents of left-libertarianism, although van Parijs eschews this label and refers to himself as a 'real-libertarian'. G. A. Cohen's writings on self-ownership, world-ownership, and equality have provided much of the inspiration for my own version of left-libertarianism, though Cohen would not describe his own views as libertarian under any modification of the term. For a definitive anthology of contemporary writings on left-libertarianism which includes contributions by each of the aforementioned see Peter Vallentyne and Hillel Steiner (eds.), *Left-Libertarianism and its Critics: The Contemporary Debate* (Basingstoke: Palgrave, 2000).

[5] John Stuart Mill, *On Liberty* (Indianapolis, Ind.: Hackett, 1978).

libertarians. At a more theoretical level, the anti-consequentialist nature of the right of self-ownership to which Lockean libertarians appeal will be congenial to those who are unconvinced by Mill's utilitarian arguments for these conclusions. Even many who would never describe themselves as libertarian find themselves in a great deal of sympathy with Nozick's non-consequentialist justification of rights as side-constraints in chapter 3 of *Anarchy, State, and Utopia*, with its emphasis on the separateness of persons and the indefensibility of the sacrificial use of persons as means for the greater good.

But I part company with Nozick in so far as I reject his claim that a right of self-ownership is incompatible with an egalitarian distribution of worldly resources. In Chapter 1 below, I argue that a robust right of self-ownership is, across a fairly wide range of individuals who differ in their capabilities, perfectly compatible with a highly egalitarian principle which calls for a distribution of worldly resources which equalizes opportunity for welfare. From within the Lockean perspective that Nozick adopts, I contend that the most defensible version of the Lockean principle of justice in acquisition of unowned resources is a strongly welfare-egalitarian one along these lines rather than the inegalitarian version which Nozick adopts. Hence, my own version of left-libertarianism is more strongly egalitarian than those which are currently well known.[6]

Following Locke, I affirm that the authority of government, when legitimate, consists of nothing more or less than the exercise of those rights over self and world which each of the governed has consented to transfer to his governor (II. 135).[7] These rights that we transfer are 'natural' rather than 'artificial' in the following sense. They are rights that do not depend for their existence on any of the following: their recognition by the laws or officials of any state or the principles of any institution; the presence of any social conventions; or the fact of any actual contractual agreement to conform one's will to the dictates of the rights.

I do not think it controversial to maintain that there are such things as natural rights and duties. For surely the injustice of murder, mayhem, or involuntary servitude is not contingent on the recognition of such injustice by the laws or officials of any state or the principles of any institution, the presence of any social conventions, or the making

---

[6] My version is, for example, more strongly egalitarian than the versions sketched in the writings of any of the four authors mentioned in n. 4 above.

[7] This notation refers to Locke's *Second Treatise of Government*, §135. Throughout this book all such references will be to the numbered sections of the *Second Treatise*.

of any actual contractual agreement. Even if people from widely different cultures were thrown together on a desert island with no sovereign or common language or custom, one person would nevertheless act contrary to duty and violate the right of another if he were to kill him for sport, to maim that person, or to enslave him against his will. One does not even need an example as mildly fantastic as the one I have just provided to make my point, since the idea of a 'crime against humanity' is familiar to us in the context of warfare. We do not need to make an enquiry into the conventions, practices, or institutions of the societies in which the Nazis or the Khmer Rouge operated, or the international laws and agreements that existed at the time, in order to condemn their atrocities. Whether or not they violated any laws, the rights and duties they violated were natural ones in the sense defined above.

It follows from this definition that a right or a duty would count as 'natural' even if both its justification and its very existence depended on the idealized *hypothetical* (as opposed to actual) contractual agreement of individuals to conform their will to the dictates of this right or duty. But, following Locke, I will not employ the device of hypothetical contractual agreement as a means of justifying rights and duties. Locke was a contractualist. But his contract was actual rather than hypothetical. Moreover, it was a means of legitimating political authority and creating political obligations rather than a means of deducing rights either in ourselves or in things.

Given the prominence of Kantian hypothetical contractualism in contemporary political philosophy, I would like briefly to explain how the method of moral reasoning about principles of justice and political legitimacy that I employ throughout this book will differ from it and why I do not take that path. Rawls is, of course, most responsible for the revival of Kantian contractualism in contemporary political philosophy.[8] But the version of contractualism that is most influential at present is Scanlon's.[9] According to Scanlon, contractualism 'holds that an act is wrong if its performance under the circumstances would be disallowed by any set of principles for the general

---

[8] See John Rawls, *A Theory of Justice* (Cambridge, Mass.: Harvard University Press, 1971).

[9] See T. M. Scanlon, *What We Owe to Each Other* (Cambridge, Mass.: Harvard University Press, 1998). Thomas Nagel, Brian Barry, and John Rawls have adopted versions of contractualism similar to Scanlon's in recent books on political philosophy (see Nagel, *Equality and Partiality* (New York: Oxford University Press, 1991), Barry, *Justice as Impartiality* (Oxford: Oxford University Press, 1995), and Rawls, *Political Liberalism* (New York: Columbia University Press, 1993)).

regulation of behavior that no one could reasonably reject as a basis for informed, unforced general agreement'.[10] Without necessarily denying that an act is wrong if it would be disallowed by principles that nobody could reasonably reject, I would want to distance myself from any accompanying claim that such a contractualist approach yields a form of reasoning about morality that is both distinct from and superior to ordinary forms of moral reasoning.[11] Rather, I believe that we need to engage in a familiar form of coherentist argumentation that appeals directly to plausible moral principles that embody substantive values to which we are committed. These principles also gain support from their ability to explain intuitions about cases and withstand the test of counter examples that appeal to our intuitions about other cases.[12] A contractualist device such as Rawls's original position that constructs principles of justice out of the self-interested choices of individuals who have been placed behind the 'veil of ignorance' will fall short of generating principles that reflect our convictions regarding the existence, importance, and stringency of natural rights of self-ownership.[13] It will fall short because, when it comes to our convictions regarding the circumstances in which it is unjust to harm others, we are moved by a variety of ethical considerations that are far too subtle to be captured by any such contractual device that reduces the choice of principle to a procedure of self-interested choice in conditions of ignorance.[14] A contractualist device such as Scanlon's that endows the parties to the contract with the ethical motivation to arrive at principles that are unreasonable to reject might, by virtue of endowing them with this motivation, ensure that the parties arrive at those principles that give natural rights their due. But this greater accuracy in choice of principles of justice is bought at the price of a reduction in

---

[10] Scanlon, *What We Owe to Each Other*, 153.

[11] To at least a certain degree, Scanlon would also distance himself from such a claim (see ibid. 241–7).

[12] Paradigm examples of this form of moral reasoning can be found in Judith Jarvis Thomson, *Rights, Restitution, and Risk* (Cambridge, Mass.: Harvard University Press, 1986), Frances Kamm, *Morality, Mortality*, 2 vols. (New York: Oxford University Press, 1993, 1996), and Warren Quinn's articles on punishment (discussed in Ch. 3 below), double effect, and doing and allowing, which are reprinted in his *Morality and Action* (Cambridge: Cambridge University Press, 1993).

[13] The details of the original position are presented in Rawls, *A Theory of Justice*, chs. 1 and 3.

[14] Frances Kamm offers a compelling explanation of why procedures that rely upon self-interested choice in conditions of ignorance would not generate the appropriate range of deontological constraints against harming. They would not, for example, generate a constraint against the sacrifice of a random innocent individual whose vital organs could be transplanted into the bodies of five who would otherwise die of a randomly distributed disease (see Kamm, *Morality, Mortality*, vol. ii).

the usefulness of the contractualist device as a means (distinct from ordinary forms of moral reasoning) of arriving at the right principles of justice. Although we can figure out what people would choose in their self-interest in conditions of ignorance without engaging in ordinary forms of moral reasoning, the same cannot be said regarding principles that would be unreasonable to reject. In order to determine which principles would be unreasonable to reject, one cannot avoid engaging in the familiar sort of moral argumentation to which I have alluded above and that I will employ throughout this book.[15]

This book divides into three parts: Part I concerns the natural rights of property in oneself and the world. Part II considers the natural rights of punishment and self-defence that form the basis, in Lockean political philosophy, for the government's authority to legislate and punish. Part III explores the nature and limits of the powers of governments which are created by the consensual transfer of the natural rights of the governed.

Part I: Self-Ownership and World-Ownership

In Chapter 1, entitled 'Self-Ownership and Equality', I delineate the nature of a libertarian right of self-ownership and argue, contrary to both Robert Nozick and G. A. Cohen, that the supposed conflict between libertarian self-ownership and equality is largely an illusion. I show how, as a matter of contingent fact, a nearly complete reconciliation of the two can in principle be achieved through a properly egalitarian understanding of the Lockean principle of justice in acquisition of worldly resources.

Chapter 2, entitled 'Making the Unjust Provide for the Disabled', deals with those circumstances in which self-ownership and equality cannot be reconciled in the manner proposed in Chapter 1. In such circumstances, I propose that liberal egalitarians and libertarians can find common ground in support of provision for the disabled by means of the coercive taxation of only those able-bodied individuals who have committed crimes.

---

[15] I acknowledge that, in some fairly limited domains, reasoning along Scanlonian contractualist lines can be illuminating. My own account in Chapter 1 of the justification of the acquisition of unowned worldly resources might strike some readers as Scanlonian. But, unlike our rights of ownership in worldly resources, I think that our rights of self-ownership cannot be given an illuminating contractualist justification of either the Scanlonian or the Rawlsian variety.

Part II: Punishment and Self-Defence

In Chapter 3, entitled 'The Right to Punish', I offer a Lockean account of a natural right to punish which is grounded in a natural right of self-protection. I endorse the essentials of Warren Quinn's derivation of the right to punish from a right of self-protection, though I argue, against Quinn, that his account will succeed only if one is allowed, when justifying punishment, to appeal to the fact that the punishment of the guilty will deter others. I also argue that Quinn's account will succeed only if the right to engage in lethal measures to protect the lives of individuals against a specified class of innocent aggressors is highly circumscribed.

In Chapter 4, entitled 'Killing the Innocent in Self-Defence', I argue in favour of such circumscription of the right to protect individuals against this class of innocent aggressors. I also argue against the right to engage in lethal measures to protect the lives of individuals against others who innocently threaten them.

Part III: Political Society

The first two chapters of Part III provide a Lockean answer to the following question: Under what conditions does a government have legitimate political authority over those whom it governs? Locke's voluntaristic answer was that such authority is derived from, and only from, the free, rational, and informed consent of the governed. Locke famously affirmed that individuals tacitly consent to the authority of a government simply by remaining within the boundaries of the territory over which the government has dominion. Such consent has often been criticized as non-binding for the distinct reasons that it is neither freely given nor offered in the appropriate circumstances of equality.

In Chapter 5, entitled 'Political Society as a Voluntary Association', I offer a reconstruction of Locke's theory of legitimate political authority which is informed by the aim of overcoming both of the aforementioned problems with his account of tacit consent. This reconstruction is left-libertarian in so far as it builds on my egalitarian interpretation in Chapter 1 of the Lockean principle of justice in acquisition of worldly resources. While remaining within the constraints of such an egalitarian principle, I endorse a highly pluralistic and decentralized account of legitimate political authority.

Even when remedied of the aforementioned problems of unfreedom and inequality, Lockean voluntarism confronts the following problem, which I address in Chapter 6 ('Left-Libertarianism versus Liberal Egalitarianism'): Lockean consent, even so remedied, would nevertheless be capable of legitimizing highly illiberal or inegalitarian political societies. Though some would regard this implication as a *reductio ad absurdum* of Lockean voluntarism, I argue to the contrary that such illiberal or inegalitarian societies would in fact be legitimized by the free and equal consent of their members. My voluntaristic account of political legitimacy which is based on actual consent therefore yields a substantive political morality that differs in crucial respects from the liberal-egalitarian Kantian hypothetical-contractualist approaches to political legitimacy that can be found in the writings of Rawls and Nagel.[16]

In Chapter 7, entitled 'The Problem of Intergenerational Sovereignty', I consider the merits of the Locke-inspired Jeffersonian idea that laws enacted by those who once lived in one's country but are now dead have no authority over the living and hence should lapse unless they are reaffirmed by a majority vote of the living. I consider and reject three attempts to justify the authority of the dead over the living. Drawing on Chapter 5, I then propose and endorse a Lockean account of how the laws of the dead can legitimately bind the living.

---

[16] Rawls, *Political Liberalism*; Nagel, *Equality and Partiality*.

PART I

Self-Ownership and World-Ownership

CHAPTER 1

Self-Ownership and Equality

G. A. Cohen has argued that the preservation in more than name only
of a libertarian right of self-ownership will come into conflict with the
realization of any strongly egalitarian principle of distributive justice,
and vice versa. One can have either self-ownership or equality only at
the cost of the virtual abandonment of the other.[1] On this point, he
and Robert Nozick are in agreement.[2] Nozick's *modus ponens* is
Cohen's *modus tollens*, since Cohen draws the conclusion that self-
ownership should give way to make room for equality, whereas
Nozick draws the opposite conclusion that equality should yield to
self-ownership.

In this chapter I argue that the conflict between libertarian self-
ownership and equality is largely an illusion. As a matter of contingent
fact, a nearly complete reconciliation of the two can be achieved
through a properly egalitarian understanding of the Lockean principle
of justice in acquisition. To put my thesis more precisely: across a
fairly wide range of individuals who differ in their capacity (productive or otherwise) to derive welfare from resources, it will be possible
in principle to distribute initially unowned worldly resources so as to
achieve equality of opportunity for welfare in a manner which is compatible with each person's possession of an uninfringed libertarian
right of self-ownership that is robust rather than merely formal.

My first task, to which I turn in Section I below, is to provide an
explanation of what libertarian self-ownership is.

---

[1] See G. A. Cohen, *Self-Ownership, Freedom, and Equality* (Cambridge: Cambridge
University Press, 1995), 15, 105.
[2] See Robert Nozick, *Anarchy, State, and Utopia* (New York: Basic Books, 1974), chs. 7 and
8, esp. pp. 167–74, 232–8.

I

> . . . every man has a *property* in his own *person*: this nobody has
> any right to but himself. The *labour* of his body, and the *work* of
> his hands, we may say, are properly his.

(II. 27)

'The central core of the notion of a property right in *X*', according to
Nozick, 'is the right to determine what shall be done with *X*'.[3] Nozick
maintains that '[t]his notion of property helps us to understand why
earlier theorists spoke of people as having property in themselves and
their labor. They viewed each person as having a right to decide what
would become of himself and what he would do, and as having a right
to reap the benefits of what he did.'[4]

Nozick condemns the egalitarian for abandoning, and commends
the libertarian for honouring, a full right of self-ownership.[5] In so far
as the libertarian endorses, while the egalitarian rejects, a stringent[6]
right to reap all of the income from one's labour, the libertarian
endorses a *fuller* right of self-ownership than the egalitarian. But does
the libertarian advocate a *full* right of self-ownership? For the purposes of answering this question, I shall adopt the following plausible
definition of a full right of self-ownership: a person's right of self-
ownership is full if and only if that person possesses, to the greatest
extent and stringency compatible with the same possession by others,
the aforementioned rights 'to decide what would become of himself
and what he would do, and . . . to reap the benefits of what he did'.[7]

---

[3] See Nozick, *Anarchy*, 171.

[4] Ibid. In this passage, Nozick appears to distinguish a right to reap the benefits of one's
labour from a right of self-ownership. In this chapter I will, if only for the sake of ease of exposition, treat a right to reap such benefits as an aspect of a right of self-ownership.

[5] Ibid. 171–2.

[6] The more stringent a right, the more difficult it is for it to be justifiably infringed in the light
of countervailing considerations that override the right. An absolute right is one that can never
be justifiably infringed. Whenever I speak of the infringement or the violation of a right, I shall
follow Judith Jarvis Thomson's use of these terms: 'Suppose that someone has a right that such
and such shall not be the case. I shall say that we infringe a right of his if and only if we bring
about that it is the case. I shall say that we violate a right of his if and only if *both* we bring about
that it is the case *and* we act wrongly in so doing' ('Some Ruminations on Rights', in Thomson,
Rights, Restitution, and Risk (Cambridge, Mass.: Harvard University Press, 1986), 51). Thomson
notes that some infringements of rights are justifiable, some are wrong but excusable, and some
are just plain wrong.

[7] Here I follow Cohen, who defines a full right of self-ownership as the 'fullest right a person
(logically) can have over herself provided that each other person also has just such a right'
(Cohen, *Self-Ownership*, 213). I should note that this notion of a 'full right of ownership' is a
technical-philosophical one that does not track the ordinary language or legal notion of 'fully
owning' something. One can, in ordinary-language terms or legally speaking, fully own a house

In defending the claim that she respects a full right of self-ownership, the libertarian must confront the following dilemma: one's possession of a full and uninfringed right of self-ownership either is or it is not compatible with some incursions upon one's body (without one's consent) that result in serious harm.

Suppose, for the sake of exposing the first horn of this dilemma, that it is not compatible with any such incursions.[8] It follows that a libertarian is, contrary to the doctrine of double effect, committed to the claim that one may not turn a trolley-car that will otherwise run over five people on to a side track where it will instead run over a sixth, and that the foreseen but unintended killing of the innocent in even a self-defensive war is never permissible.[9] The libertarian is also committed to the claim that one acts impermissibly if by one's actions one unforeseeably kills or injures an innocent, non-threatening person even though what one did was not known to carry a risk of harm, or the known risk of harm associated with the activity was so minuscule that most would deem the activity justifiable.[10] On this construal of a full right of self-ownership, a libertarian can maintain that she holds the morally pure, principled, and uncompromising position that our rights of self-ownership are full only at the price of a hitherto under-emphasized moral fanaticism. The fanaticism of which I speak is not the oft-noted fanaticism of a libertarian that rules out even the most trivial amount of forced labour or taxation for the purpose of alleviating a great deal of misery. Rather, it is a fanaticism that rules out any seriously harmful incursions whatsoever upon the bodies of innocents, even when such incursions are merely foreseen as a necessary by-product of the minimization of harm rather than intended as a means of minimizing harm, and even when they are the unforeseen result of activities that carry either no known or the most minuscule

that one cannot destroy because it is a historical landmark even though it is both plausible to hold and a consequence of the definition I have just introduced that one's right of ownership over that house is less full than it would have been if, *ceteris paribus*, one had the right to destroy it.

[8] Cohen maintains that it is not compatible with any such incursions (see ibid. 227).

[9] Libertarians do not object to harming villainous aggressors in self-defence or punishing them. But those harmed might plausibly be regarded as having forfeited their full right of self-ownership. (Note that Nozick believes that it is also permissible to kill *innocent* threats and aggressors in self-defence and flirts with the idea that it is permissible to kill innocent shields of threats as well (see Nozick, *Anarchy*, 34–5). It is difficult to justify such self-defensive killings by an appeal to forfeiture.)

[10] Nozick, however, claims that it is permissible to impose risks of death on another. He is favourably disposed to the view that one may act permissibly even if one ends up killing another person without fully compensating him for being killed (see ibid. 77–8). Nozick also claims that it is permissible unforeseeably to kill in some cases, since a ban on such killing would place one at too much risk and fear of being imprisoned on account of events beyond one's control (see ibid. 71).

known risk of doing harm.[11] Such fanaticism is, moreover, unnecessary in so far as the libertarian could permit such unintentional incursions without also having to abandon her opposition to redistributive taxation for the purposes of promoting equality. This is because the libertarian's case against redistributive taxation is premissed upon a right against being used as a means by being forced (via incursions or threats of incursions upon one's mind and body) to sacrifice life, limb, or labour.[12] It is not premissed upon a right against harmful incursions upon one's body *simpliciter*.

Now suppose, for the sake of exposing the other horn of the dilemma, that one's possession of a full and uninfringed right of self-ownership is compatible with some incursions upon one's body (without one's consent) that result in serious harm. In this case, the libertarian must explain why these incursions, but not others that the libertarian denounces as violations of a full right of self-ownership, are compatible with such a right. The libertarian must explain why, for example, one does not violate someone's full right of self-ownership if one kills him in the trolley-car case, yet one does if one kills him in order to transplant his vital organs. But I do not think such an explanation is possible.[13]

[11] Could a libertarian climb off this horn of the dilemma by holding that such cases involve infringements of rights that are in the final analysis morally justifiable (or at least excusable)? I think not, since the dilemma is about what is compatible with a full right of self-ownership, where this is defined as one that is of maximal universalizable stringency. A right that is not so stringent as to condemn such infringements (i.e. violations) would not be of maximal universalizable stringency. Moreover, one is open to the charge of moral fanaticism even if one holds that these infringements are unjustifiable but excusable.

[12] Nozick says that libertarian 'constraints upon action reflect the underlying Kantian principle that individuals are ends and not merely means; they may not be sacrificed or used for the achieving of other ends without their consent' (Nozick, *Anarchy*, 30–1). I shall discuss his case against redistributive taxation below.

[13] Nozick attempts such an explanation simply by asserting that a right of self-ownership is full if it fills all of the logical space *within the boundaries* set by the libertarian constraints against aggression that people possess. He maintains that a property right in X is 'the right to choose which of the constrained set of options concerning X shall be realized or attempted. The constraints are set by other principles or laws operating in the society; in our theory, by the Lockean rights people possess (under the minimal state)' (ibid. 171). These constraints condemn some, but not all, bodily incursions that result in serious harm. In so bounding his right of self-ownership, Nozick opens himself up to the following egalitarian rejoinder: 'So long as the fullness of rights of self-ownership is a matter of filling all the space inside moral "constraints [that] are set by other principles or laws operating in the society", I too can show that I respect a full right of self-ownership simply by bounding our rights of ownership by (among other rights and duties) the rights of others to our assistance (financial and otherwise) and our correlative duties to assist.' If Nozick's notion of self-ownership is full only because it presupposes libertarian rather than egalitarian rights and duties, he cannot offer a defence of libertarianism over egalitarianism on the grounds that it respects, but egalitarianism denies, a full right of self-ownership. That just amounts to a tendentious defence of libertarianism on the grounds that it respects, and egalitarianism rejects, libertarian constraints.

The libertarian position that I consider in this chapter avoids this dilemma because it is not committed to a full right of self-ownership. I shall define a 'libertarian right of self-ownership' as one that, while less than full because it does not prohibit all unintentional incursions upon one's body, encompasses the following two rights:[14]

(1) A very stringent right of control over and use of one's mind and body that bars others from intentionally using one as a means by forcing one to sacrifice life, limb, or labour, where such force operates by means of incursions or threats of incursions upon one's mind and body (including assault and battery and forcible arrest, detention, and imprisonment).[15]

(2) A very stringent right to all of the income that one can gain from one's mind and body (including one's labour) either on one's own or through unregulated and untaxed voluntary exchanges with other individuals.[16]

Egalitarians who are also liberals would say that they are happy to endorse the first of the two libertarian rights of self-ownership just enumerated.[17] Liberal egalitarians would express agreement with libertarians that individuals possess stringent rights of ownership over their bodies that stand in the way of their being used as means by being forced to donate vital bodily organs such as a heart or a liver, or being forced to donate non-vital body parts or products such as an eye or a kidney, or blood or bone marrow.[18] Liberal egalitarians would also

[14] An analysis of the concept of a libertarian right of self-ownership in terms of such rights should lay to rest worries about the coherence of this concept. Brian Barry presses such worries in his review of Cohen's book entitled 'You Have to Be Crazy to Believe It', *TLS*, 25 Oct. 1996, 28. Cohen responds in the *TLS*, 8 Nov. 1996, 19. I concede that talk of property in persons might strike some modern ears as an artificial and unwarranted extension of the concept of property. But nothing will be lost if those who resist such talk simply mentally delete the words 'property' or 'ownership' throughout this book and replace them with an assertion of the relevant rights.

[15] The notion of 'using as a means', though intuitive, has proved resistant to philosophical analysis. The best analysis I know of is in Warren Quinn's 'Actions, Intentions, and Consequences: The Doctrine of Double Effect', *Philosophy and Public Affairs*, 18 (1989): 334–51.

[16] As will become clear below, these rights must be exercised within the confines of our rights of world-ownership.

[17] I take Rawls and Dworkin to be exemplars of liberal egalitarianism (see John Rawls, *A Theory of Justice* (Cambridge, Mass.: Harvard University Press, 1971) and Ronald Dworkin, *Sovereign Virtue* (Cambridge, Mass.: Harvard University Press, 2000)).

[18] The right not to be forced to donate an eye or a kidney, or blood or bone marrow, extends beyond a right against the sorts of painful and invasive incursions upon (other parts of) one's body which might be necessary in order to force such giving. For suppose that in order to preserve the functioning of one of one's eyes or kidneys it must be temporarily removed and then reimplanted after it has been treated. One would still have a strong right of control over the disposition of that organ between the point of removal and reimplantation, and such a right could not be explained by an appeal to one's right against painful and invasive incursions upon (other parts of) one's body.

profess agreement with libertarians that individuals possess stringent rights of self-ownership that stand in the way of their being used as means by being forced via threat of imprisonment to work for the sake of the good of others.

Although they affirm the first of the two libertarian rights of self-ownership, liberal egalitarians typically reject the second, which is widely regarded as prima facie far less compelling than the first.[19] Yet Nozick has argued that this second right follows from the first. He has famously argued that '[t]axation of earning from labor is on a par with forced labor'.[20] If Nozick's complaint against redistributive taxation is correct, then, in so far as egalitarianism is achieved through a redistributive tax on income, it will infringe a right against forced labour that liberal egalitarians claim to recognize.

In Section II below I show that Nozick's argument is not essentially a complaint that such taxation is on a par with forced labour but rather the complaint that such taxation violates one's rights of ownership *simpliciter*. Furthermore, I show that, with the exception of cases in which we need not make use of worldly resources in order to perform labour, Nozick's argument relies upon a suppressed and controversial premiss regarding the justifiability of inequality-generating rights of ownership over the world. Having exposed this premiss, I reject it in Section III in favour of a welfare-egalitarian Lockean account of our rights of ownership over the world. In Sections IV–V I show how such an egalitarianism need not come into conflict with an uninfringed libertarian right of self-ownership that is, moreover, robust rather than merely formal.

II

In order to assess Nozick's claim that redistributive taxation is on a par with forced labour, we need to consider the various ways in which one can generate income from one's labour. One can generate income with or without performing labour on worldly resources and with or without engaging in trade with others. These two distinctions generate the possibilities shown in Fig. 1. Most forms of income-generating labour

[19] John Christman, for example, has attacked those aspects of libertarian self-ownership that he calls 'income rights', which include the right to benefit from the exchange of one's labour for goods. But he endorses those aspects of self-ownership that he calls 'control rights', which include rights against injury and forced labour (see Christman, 'Self-Ownership, Equality, and the Structure of Property Rights', *Political Theory*, 19 (1991): 28–46).

[20] Nozick, *Anarchy*, 169. More precisely, he says (ibid.) that 'taking the earnings of *n* hours of labor . . . is like forcing the person to work *n* hours for another's purpose'.

involve the use of worldly resources. A paradigmatic case of such labour is farming, which involves ploughing soil, planting seeds, watering, and harvesting crops. Some forms of income-generating labour do not, however, involve the use of worldly resources. Performing a song and dance for a paying audience in a public place is one example. In the case of most labour one can generate income through trading: the farmer can trade crops for other commodities or for money, and the performer can trade her entertainment for money. One does not, however, always need to engage in trading in order to generate income. The farmer can generate an income that consists of the food that she harvests even if she never trades with anybody else, where income is to be understood, in the context of this discussion, as any beneficial material goods that one gains as the result of one's labour. It is more difficult to imagine cases in which one might gain income, so defined, in the absence of trading as the result of labour that does not involve worldly resources. One example is the weaving together of loose strands of one's hair into a toupee to cover one's bald spot or into clothing to keep oneself warm.

	Worldly resources	No worldly resources
Trading	e.g. Farming	e.g. Entertaining
No trading	e.g. Farming	e.g. Hair weaving

Fig. 1 Means of generating income from labour

In assessing Nozick's argument that redistributive taxation is on a par with forced labour, I will first consider a rather bizarre case that does not involve the use of worldly resources. It is important to consider such a case in isolation from cases that involve worldly resources, since it is only in cases that do not involve worldly resources that Nozick's objection to redistributive taxation is very persuasive.[21] Nozick's objection to redistributive taxation in general is persuasive only if one mistakenly assimilates cases that involve worldly resources with cases that do not.

---

[21] Cf. Cohen, *Self-Ownership*, 170 n. 10, where he envisions a scenario in which there are no worldly resources for people to exploit: 'people float in space, and all necessary and luxury services take the form of other people touching them in various ways'. He maintains that 'it is far more difficult to object to inequality in this world than it is to object to it' in a world in which differences in welfare are solely a function of differential access to worldly resources.

Imagine a highly artificial 'society' of two strangers, each of whom will freeze to death unless clothed. Unfortunately, the only source of material for clothing is human hair, which can be woven into clothing. One of the two is hirsute and capable of weaving, whereas the other is bald and incapable of weaving. The weaver would, however, prefer to weave only one set of clothing for herself and none for the other person. The 'state' (which we might imagine to be a third person with enforcement powers but no needs of her own) imposes a 50 per cent income tax on the weaver by declaring that she must give half of whatever she chooses to weave to the non-weaver. If she does not do so of her own accord, then the state will literally force her to do so by seizing that which she owes in tax and giving it to the non-weaver.

There is a clear sense in which this tax forces the weaver to work for the sake of the non-weaver. She will, after all, freeze to death if she does not work at all. But if she works then she must weave one out of every two articles of clothing not for her own sake, but for the sake of the non-weaver. She must, therefore, on pain of freezing to death, spend half of her time working for the sake of the non-weaver.[22]

But not all schemes of redistributive taxation force those who are taxed to work for the sake of others on pain of death. The state could instead refrain from imposing any redistributive tax until a fairly high level of income has been reached. It could, for example, tax the weaver only on the items she produces that are surplus to a sizeable wardrobe which she has woven for her own benefit. Nozick is opposed to such a 'luxury income tax'. He believes that it, no less than a 'necessity income tax', amounts to forced labour.[23] Yet such a tax cannot literally constitute forced labour, since it would be so easy to avoid. To illustrate this point, consider the following pair of cases that are analogous to a necessity income tax and a luxury income tax at least in so far as the question of forced labour is concerned. In the first, a thug orders you to be his slave for the afternoon on pain of death. In the second, a thug announces that you must be a slave for the afternoon if and only if you now hum a certain song that you happen to have no particular desire to hum. In the first case, he forces you to be his slave for the afternoon. In the second, he does not. In both cases, however, you have a decisive complaint against the thug: that by his threats he vio-

---

[22] I should, however, note that Nozick denies that the fact that someone must work on pain of death is a sufficient condition of forced labour, since he denies that the propertyless worker who must work on pain of starvation is forced to work (see Nozick, *Anarchy*, 262–5).

[23] In the case of any system of redistributive taxation, according to Nozick, the 'fact that others intentionally intervene, in violation of a side constraint against aggression, to threaten force to limit the alternatives [that would be open to the taxed individual if the tax were not imposed], makes the taxation system one of forced labor' (ibid. 169).

lates your property right to do as you choose with that which is rightfully yours (yourself in both cases).

These observations demonstrate that Nozick's complaint against redistributive taxation is not essentially a complaint about being forced to work. Rather, it is essentially an objection to the violation of property rights. Nozick's complaint against the imposition of a luxury income tax on the weaver must be grounded in the claim that she has not forfeited her rights to, but rather legitimately owns, that which she has used to weave and has woven, and that a redistributive income tax would violate her rights of ownership in these things. The weaver's rights of ownership over her means of production and the fruits of her labour can plausibly be grounded solely and completely in her libertarian right of self-ownership. Her means of production consist of nothing more than her mind and parts of her body, and the fruits of her labour consist of nothing more than parts of her body that have been transformed into items that are suitable to be worn as clothing. In order to rebut the libertarian's objection to taxation in this instance, the egalitarian must hold either that the weaver does not possess a libertarian right of self-ownership or that this right is not as stringent as the libertarian thinks it is and may justifiably be infringed in these circumstances. But this is to acknowledge that if there is such a thing as a libertarian right of self-ownership, then it comes into conflict with equality in these circumstances. If the imposition of a luxury income tax on the weaver were both necessary and sufficient to prevent another human being from freezing to death, opponents of libertarianism could justifiably hold that only an unreasonably fanatical devotee of a right of self-ownership could insist that such a right is so stringent that it rules out the imposition of this tax. But I believe that the libertarian gains the upper hand when the opponent goes so far as to claim that a tax may be imposed on the weaver not merely in order to ensure that the non-weaver does not freeze to death or is able to enjoy a certain amount of comfort, but in order to ensure that the non-weaver end up with a wardrobe that is no less luxurious than the weaver's.[24] The libertarian's case against this latter tax is strong.[25]

[24] Except perhaps for that which is necessary to compensate the weaver for the disutility of labour of which she alone is capable.

[25] If, *contra* the egalitarian, Nozick's argument soundly condemns taxation for the purposes of realizing an egalitarian distribution as a violation of one's property rights in self, why doesn't it similarly condemn taxation for the purposes of providing for the national defence, police protection, and the judicial system? A libertarian does not object to coercive taxation for these purposes. But here one is forced to pay for goods that one has received. In this respect, this case is analogous to the government's unobjectionable forcing of an individual to work to pay off her credit-card bill for goods that she has contracted to receive on promise of later payment. In the

So far the property rights that the redistributive tax is thought by the libertarian to violate have involved only rights of self-ownership. We have not yet considered cases in which one needs to make use of the world in order to earn income. But when, as is often the case in actual fact, one must make use of the world in order to earn income, Nozick's complaint against redistributive taxation is much more difficult to get off the ground. Consider the case of a farmer who is forced by the government, on pain of imprisonment, to give half of whatever income she earns from farming to hungry orphans. This case might seem morally to be on a par with the case of the weaver who must give half of whatever she earns from weaving to the needy. But they are, in fact, on a par only if the following premiss is true: in addition to having a right of self-ownership that is as full as the weaver's, she also possesses a right of ownership over the land that she farms that is as full as her right of ownership over herself. Although Nozick is elsewhere sensitive to the need to justify world-ownership, nowhere in his argument against redistributive taxation does he disclose that his complaint relies on the following generalized version of this premiss: that one's right of ownership over worldly resources that one uses in order to earn income is as full as one's right of ownership over oneself.[26] Were the farmer to possess such a right of ownership over land, then the tax would be at the very least a justifiable infringement of and at worst an unjustifiable violation of her rights of ownership. But if the farmer's

case of the goods of national defence, etc. one never entered into any voluntary agreement. Nevertheless, one has received goods. I believe that payment for these goods can often be justified by the 'principle of fairness', according to which one may be forced to pay for 'public goods' from which one has benefited and which it is impossible selectively to exclude people from receiving. (Nozick, however, rejects any appeal to the principle of fairness (see his discussion of this principle in Nozick, *Anarchy*, 90–5)).

[26] That it relies upon this premiss is a point to which Cohen is oddly insensitive. I say 'insensitive' because Cohen affirms that redistributive taxation conflicts with libertarian self-ownership. Yet he does not supply the qualification that it need not conflict in cases in which one must labour upon worldly resources in order to earn income and one's rights of ownership over these resources is not as full as one's right of ownership over oneself. (For both the affirmation and failure to qualify see Cohen, *Self-Ownership*, 216–21, 240.) I say 'oddly' because it was he who demonstrated that libertarian self-ownership among the unequally talented does not by itself imply inequality in holdings. One must conjoin a premiss of self-ownership with an inegalitarian premiss of world-ownership in order to reach this result—see ibid. chs. 3–4, esp. pp. 112–15. These chapters are revisions of a pair of pioneering articles entitled 'Self-Ownership, World-Ownership, and Equality' and 'Self-Ownership, World-Ownership, and Equality: Part II'. The former appeared in Frank Lucash (ed.), *Justice and Equality Here and Now* (Ithaca, NY: Cornell University Press, 1986) and the latter appeared in *Social Philosophy and Philosophy*, 3 (1986): 77–96. These articles drew attention to the centrality of a right of self-ownership to Nozick's political philosophy. They also prepared the way, without travelling down it, to a proper understanding of the relationship between self-ownership and equality as mediated by world-ownership.

right of ownership over the land she farms were less full, then the tax on her income would involve a lesser infringement of her property rights. If, for example, the farmer had voluntarily purchased the land she farms from someone on the condition that she give half of her harvest to the needy, then the state would do no wrong by stepping in to force her to give this portion away to the needy. Such force would not even infringe (much less violate) any property right of the farmer's but rather would be a justifiable means of enforcing a voluntary contractual obligation. Similarly, if the farmer had stolen all of the land she farms, the state would be justified in confiscating some of the product of her labour and giving it, as well as the land, back to the rightful owner in compensation for the theft. Such confiscation would not even infringe (much less violate) any right of the thief.

Egalitarians correctly question whether there could be a moral presumption analogous to that of a libertarian right of self-ownership in the case of the farmer's title over her land, since a presumption in favour of such a right of ownership over any bit of land has a good deal less prima-facie plausibility than a presumption in favour of such a right of ownership over self.[27] Perhaps even if we possess a libertarian right of ownership over ourselves, we can only ever come to have a less full right of ownership over land and other worldly resources. Perhaps we can come to own any bit of land or other worldly resource only on the condition that we share some of whatever we reap from it with others. If this were true, then the state's forcing each of us to share our harvest with others would be no more an infringement of a libertarian right of self-ownership than in the case in which one purchased a plot of land from someone else on the condition that one share a part of one's harvest with the needy. Perhaps there are other moral limitations to our rights of ownership over worldly resources which make them less extensive than libertarian rights of self-ownership. Alternatively, we might be entitled to acquire rights of ownership over land and other worldly resources that are as full as the libertarian right of self-ownership. But this entitlement might only extend to such acquisition

[27] Cf. Cohen: '[O]ne may plausibly say . . . of raw land and worldly resources (out of which all unraw external things are, be it noted, made), that no person has, at least to begin with, a greater right in them than any other does; whereas the same thought is less compelling when it is applied to human parts and powers. Jean-Jacques Rousseau described the original formation of private property as a usurpation of what should be freely accessible to all, and many have found his thesis persuasive, but few would discern a comparable injustice in a person's insistence on sovereignty over his own limbs' (Cohen, *Self-Ownership*, 71).

I completely endorse the above passage. As will become clear in the next section, however, I do not myself affirm what Cohen says one may plausibly say, nor do I count myself among the many who have found Rousseau's thesis persuasive.

as is consistent with the realization of equality. I will explore some of these possibilities in the sections that follow.

III

Under what conditions can one come to have rights of ownership over bits of the world? To answer this question I will, in this section and the next, consider hypothetical cases in which childless adults with no worldly resources on their persons have washed ashore on an uninhabited and undiscovered and therefore unowned island.[28] I believe, and argue in Section V, that the principle of justice in acquisition that applies in such cases is directly relevant to the question of justice in the holdings of members of contemporary societies.

I endorse a Lockean principle of justice in acquisition of previously unowned worldly resources which maintains that an individual can come to acquire rights of ownership over a previously unowned bit of the world if and only if such acquisition places nobody else at a disadvantage. Such acquisition that leaves 'enough and as good' for others to acquire is justified because it is 'no prejudice to any others' (II. 33).[29]

Nozick would, I think, concur that one can acquire property rights

---

[28] Locke, however, appears to be committed to the denial of this inference. He claims 'that God gave the world to *Adam*, and his posterity in common' (II. 25). Moreover, he thinks that this gift implies a 'right and power over the earth and inferior creatures in common' (Locke, *Two Treatises of Government*, ed. Peter Laslett (Cambridge: Cambridge University Press, 1988), bk. I, §67). This right is a property right. Here I follow A. John Simmons, *The Lockean Theory of Rights* (Princeton, NJ: Princeton University Press, 1992), 239–40. But in the absence of any such belief that the earth was previously owned by some being who transferred this right of ownership to humankind at the outset, it is reasonable to regard the earth as initially unowned.

[29] In order to come to acquire such rights of ownership that place nobody else at a disadvantage, there must have been some method of acquisition. For Locke, the method consists of the mixing of one's labour with worldly resources (II. 27–35). But on my own account the method need not involve the mixing of one's labour with any bit of the world. It can instead involve the mere staking of a claim. Labouring on something may be a way of staking a claim. But it ought not to be the only way, since, if it were, then incapacitated individuals who are incapable of mixing any of their labour with worldly resources would be unfairly deprived of any method of acquiring resources which might nevertheless be useful to them. They ought to be entitled to stake a claim simply by publicly proclaiming the boundaries of the worldly resources over which they claim rights of ownership. Perhaps the mere staking of a claim that does not leave others at a disadvantage would not be sufficient to generate a property right. One might need to add that the resources in question must be of some use to the claim-staker, where 'use' is read broadly to include the benefit one could derive from trading them for something else or from investing them. (Even if the planet Neptune never was and never will become of any use to anyone, and hence my coming to own it will not place anyone at a disadvantage, it seems odd to say that I come to own it simply by staking a claim to it by means of public proclamation.) I will ignore this qualification and will concern myself only with the staking of claims on resources that are of some use.

in previously unowned worldly resources so long as such acquisition does not place others at a disadvantage.[30] His version of the Lockean proviso runs as follows:

> *Nozick's proviso.* You may acquire previously unowned land (and its fruits) if and only if you make nobody else worse off than she would have been in a state of nature in which no land is privately held but each is free to gather and consume food and water from the land and make use of it.[31]

As a means of ensuring that nobody is placed at a disadvantage, Nozick's version of the Lockean proviso is too weak, since it allows a single individual in a state of nature to engage in an enriching acquisition of all the land there is if she compensates all others by hiring them and paying a wage that ensures that they end up no worse off than they would have been if they had continued to live the meagre hand-to-mouth existence of hunters and gatherers on non-private land.[32] Such acquisition would pre-empt others from making any acquisitions of their own that would improve their situation over that in which they live no better than a meagre hand-to-mouth existence. This acquisition is objectionable both because it condemns others to such a miserable existence and because it is manifestly unfair that a first grabber be allowed to monopolize all opportunities to improve one's lot through acquisition. The charge of unfairness would be mitigated somewhat if each person had a genuinely equal chance to engage in such first-grabbing (as they would if, for example, permission to grab first were determined by lot). But Nozick's proviso permits first-grabbing even when chances are not equal. And even if his proviso were modified so as to permit first-grabbing only when chances were equal, the following weaker complaint of unfairness would remain: the modified proviso has the consequence that someone will have the opportunity to acquire a much greater share of resources than others as the result of factors beyond the control of individuals. Such an equal chance to grab

---

[30] See Nozick, *Anarchy*, 174–82.

[31] Some of the language in Nozick's text points to a more demanding formulation of the proviso along the following lines: 'You may acquire previously unowned land (and its fruits) if and only if you make nobody else worse off than she would have been if she had instead been free to gather and consume food and water from this land and make use of it but not to privatize the land itself.' The counter example to Nozick's proviso that I present below applies to this formulation as well as the one in the main text above. For a discussion of the differing implications of these two formulations see Jonathan Wolff, *Robert Nozick* (Palo Alto, Calif.: Stanford University Press, 1991), 112.

[32] Cohen is the inventor of this counter example to Nozick's proviso (see Cohen, *Self-Ownership*, ch. 3).

first might be entirely fair and appropriate in unusual circumstances in which the lion's share of worldly resources cannot be divided and will therefore go to waste unless a single person is allowed to acquire such a large share. But when resources are more evenly divisible, any principle of 'winner-takes-the-lion's-share' is prima facie less fair than a principle of acquisition which gives rise to a more equal distribution of resources.

The following version of the Lockean proviso provides a remedy to these defects in Nozick's version:

Egalitarian proviso. You may acquire previously unowned worldly resources if and only if you leave enough so that everyone else[33] can acquire an equally advantageous share of unowned worldly resources.[34]

The egalitarian proviso has prima-facie plausibility for the following reason: One's coming to acquire previously unowned resources under these terms leaves nobody else at a disadvantage (or, in Locke's words, is 'no prejudice to any others'), where being left at a disadvantage is understood as being left with less than an equally advantageous share of resources. Any weaker, less egalitarian versions of the proviso would, like Nozick's, unfairly allow some to acquire greater advantage than others from their acquisition of unowned land and other worldly resources.[35]

[33] Excluding those who have already acquired an equally advantageous share of unowned worldly resources. Those who have already acquired a less than equally advantageous share should be left with enough so that they can acquire that which, in combination with what they have already acquired, constitutes an equally advantageous share.

[34] I ignore further qualifications that would be needed to take account of the following considerations. Perhaps certain especially magnificent stretches of wilderness should never be fully privatized. Even in the absence of such magnificent wilderness, perhaps a certain portion of the earth should be kept in reserve for common ownership. This might be justified on the grounds that people value public spaces that are unconditionally open to all—public spaces which are public goods in the economist's sense. The per-capita value of land to those who commonly own it must be taken into account in determining each person's rightful share of worldly resources. This raises tricky questions, which I will not attempt to answer here, having to do with the value to different people of commonly owned land.

[35] A defender of inequality might reply that any complaint of unfairness or injustice would be silenced in the case of an unequal distribution in which everybody enjoys greater advantage than he would have enjoyed under an equal distribution and the greater advantage redounds to the maximal benefit of the least well off. I do not think such complaints would necessarily be silenced. Cohen, for example, has convincingly argued that some such inequalities which Rawls's difference principle permits would be unjust (see Cohen, 'Incentives, Inequality, and Community', in Grethe B. Peterson (ed.), *The Tanner Lectures on Human Values*, xiii (Salt Lake City, Utah: University of Utah Press, 1992), and 'The Pareto Argument for Inequality', *Social Philosophy and Policy*, 12 (1995): 160–85).

The phrase 'equally advantageous shares of unowned worldly resources' that I employ in the egalitarian proviso should be read as a term of art that is neutral among a range of familiar welfarist and resource-based metrics of equality.[36] Some would say that shares are equally advantageous if they are such that none would prefer to trade her bundle of worldly resources with anybody else's.[37] Others would say that shares are equally advantageous if they are such that none would prefer to trade the sum of her bundle of worldly resources and personal resources (where the latter consists of one's mental and physical capacities).[38] And others would say that shares are equally advantageous if they are such that each is able to attain the same level of welfare as anybody else given the combination of her worldly and personal resources.[39]

In the discussion which follows I shall adopt the latter welfarist specification of the egalitarian proviso, since I believe that an opportunity-for-welfare metric most convincingly realizes the aforementioned value of fairness which underpins the egalitarian proviso. Before spelling out the details of this welfarist specification, I would like to make a preliminary appeal to intuitions about some cases in order to motivate the claim that egalitarian justice calls for the equalization of opportunity for welfare rather than the equalization of anything other than, or in addition to, that.

---

[36] Compare this phrasing with the phrasing of Hillel Steiner's egalitarian interpretation of the Lockean proviso: '*each individual has a right to an equal share of the basic non-human means of production*' (Steiner, 'The Natural Right to the Means of Production', *Philosophical Quarterly*, 27 (1977): 41–9, at 49). Note that Steiner affirms an entitlement to an 'equal share', whereas I affirm an entitlement to an 'equally advantageous share'. I have chosen this latter phrasing because it is relatively neutral between welfarist and resource-based specifications of the egalitarian metric. Steiner's phrasing, by contrast, lends itself to a resource-based specification of the egalitarian metric, and he in fact endorses such a specification. (See also n. 46 below.)

[37] See Steiner, 'Capitalism, Justice, and Equal Starts', *Social Philosophy and Policy*, 5 (1987): 49–71.

[38] See Dworkin, 'Do Liberty and Equality Conflict?' in Paul Barker (ed.), *Living as Equals* (Oxford: Oxford University Press, 1996), 45–8. See also Dworkin, *Sovereign Virtue*, 80–92, 140–1.

[39] Following Richard Arneson, I will call this metric 'equality of opportunity for welfare' (see Arneson, 'Equality and Equality of Opportunity for Welfare', *Philosophical Studies*, 56 (1989): 77–93). Roughly speaking, I understand people to have equal opportunity for welfare if and only if the levels of welfare that people have attained differ only as the result of choices for which they can be held morally responsible. (Here I adopt Cohen's definition of 'equality of access to advantage' (see Cohen, 'On the Currency of Egalitarian Justice', *Ethics*, 99 (1989): 906–44, at 916).) Arneson (ibid.) and Cohen (ibid.) persuasively argue that, by rendering one's level of advantage sensitive to choices for which one can be held morally responsible, the equalization of *opportunity* rather than *outcome* reflects a concern for fairness. This point holds irrespective of whether advantage is measured in terms of welfare, resources, or something else.

A reflection on cases such as the following supports the notion that a fair share of worldly resources is plausibly measured in terms of equality of opportunity for welfare rather than equality of opportunity for worldly resources. Suppose that the only worldly resource available for use by each of two individuals who are stranded on a desert island is an unowned large blanket that can be divided into portions of any size. If the blanket did not exist, then both would freeze to death. One of these individuals is, through no fault of his, twice as large as the other. If the blanket is divided into equally large portions, then the smaller of the two will have enough to enjoy the luxury of being able to wrap the blanket around himself twice, whereas the larger of the two will suffer the (non-life-or-limb-threatening) discomfort of partial exposure to the cold because he will be able to cover only a portion of his body. The blanket could, however, be divided into unequal portions that enable each to cover his entire body once, thereby leaving them equally comfortable. (But neither is as comfortable as he would have been if he had a greater share of the blanket.) Intuitively, it would be unfair for the smaller person to acquire half of the blanket rather than that lesser portion which would leave him as comfortable as the other.[40]

Cases can, however, also be constructed which strongly suggest that welfarist considerations do not exhaust the potential for egalitarian justice. Ronald Dworkin has persuasively argued that a legitimate claim for resources to compensate for disabilities can be made even in the case of those who are no worse off in terms of opportunity for welfare than anyone else. Dickens's Tiny Tim has a legitimate claim for a greater than equal share of worldly resources to compensate for his disability even if his opportunity for welfare would be the same as everyone else's under an equal division of worldly resources and higher than others' as the result of such a transfer of resources to him.[41] I am moved by the claim that disabilities merit transfers of resources even in the case of those who would not suffer a deficit in their opportunity for welfare in the absence of such transfers. I therefore think the welfare-egalitarian proviso might need to be qualified to

---

[40] I should note that the welfare here in question is fairly purely sensation-based rather than judgement-mediated. In other words, the welfare is fairly purely a matter of one's level of physical comfort rather than a matter of preferences which reflect one's judgement about what is and is not valuable. Special problems for welfare egalitarianism arise in the case of such things as expensive tastes which reflect such judgements. Dworkin has ably exposed such problems in *Sovereign Virtue*, ch. 1. For a defence of the welfare metric against Dworkin's critique see Cohen, 'On the Currency'. For a reply to Cohen see Dworkin, *Sovereign Virtue*, ch. 7. For a rebuttal of Dworkin's reply see Cohen, 'Expensive Taste Rides Again', unpublished.

[41] See Dworkin, *Sovereign Virtue*, ch. 1.

allow departures from equality of opportunity for welfare which such compensation for disabilities would necessitate. But, unlike Cohen, I would not draw the more general conclusion from reflection on cases such as that of Tiny Tim that compensation for unchosen differences in mental and physical abilities as such is one of the aims of egalitarian justice.[42] This is because I think the claim to compensate for certain unchosen disabilities does not generalize to a claim to compensate for all unchosen differences in abilities as such. To see why, let us consider the case of Deft Tim who, while much more fleet and nimble of foot than others who are all merely ordinarily deft, is just as well off as anyone else in terms of opportunity for welfare under an equal division of worldly resources. Suppose that everyone in this society, including Deft Tim, would prefer Deft Tim's extraordinary deftness to the ordinary deftness of the rest. Cohen would call for a transfer of resources from Deft Tim to the ordinarily deft simply in order to compensate for the inequality in their deftness. Deft Tim should, according to him, end up with less opportunity for welfare and fewer resources than others simply in order to redress the fact that he is more adroit than they. But I do not think that the ordinarily deft have any claim on Deft Tim's resources simply to compensate for the difference in capacity between them and him. It is, I think, only when people's lesser capacities fall short of the level of normal human functioning that a sound non-welfarist case can be made for compensating those whose capacities are lower than other's.

I shall now spell out the details of my preferred welfarist specification of the egalitarian proviso. According to this specification, the phrase 'equally advantageous share of unowned worldly resources' that occurs in the egalitarian proviso should be understood as follows:

> *Welfarist specification of the egalitarian proviso.* Someone else's share is as advantageous as yours if and only if it is such that she would be able (by producing, consuming, or trading) to better herself to the same degree as you, where 'betterment' is to be measured in terms of level of welfare understood as the 'satisfaction of the self-interested preferences that the individual would have after ideal deliberation while thinking clearly with full pertinent information regarding those preferences'.[43]

---

[42] Cohen has argued that the correct metric of egalitarian justice consists of a hybrid of opportunity for welfare, opportunity for worldly resources, and physical and mental capacities (see Cohen, 'On the Currency').

[43] The quoted words are Arneson's formulation of the preference-satisfaction conception of welfare (see Arneson, 'Primary Goods Reconsidered', *Noûs*, 24 (1990): 429–54, at 448). For further elaboration of this conception of welfare see also Arneson, 'Liberalism, Distributive

The phrase 'to the same degree' can be interpreted either as 'by the same increment of increase in welfare' or 'to the same absolute level of welfare'. In adjudicating between these two interpretations, I will be guided by the following more fundamental moral principle: one is entitled to acquire worldly resources so long as one's acquisition does not give rise to a legitimate complaint on the part of anybody else.[44] Let us assume, for the purposes of adjudication, a two-person island whose resources are of uniform quality and unowned at the outset. The two inhabitants, Alpha and Beta, are equal in their mental and physical capacities, including their productive talents, and they derive equal welfare per unit of resources consumed. They would also both be comfortably well off in terms of welfare in the absence of any resources. There is, however, one crucial difference between the two. As luck would have it, Alpha would be less well off than Beta in the absence of any resources simply on account of differences in their physical and mental constitution.[45] One further assumption: if Alpha were to acquire all of the island's resources, leaving Beta with none, then he would end up equally well off in terms of opportunity for welfare as Beta. Therefore, were Alpha to acquire all of the island's resources, this would give rise to a state of affairs in which nobody is worse off in terms of opportunity for welfare than anybody else. On the 'equal-absolute-level' reading, the proviso would be uniquely satisfied by such a distribution. On the 'equal-increment-of-increase' reading, by contrast, the proviso be satisfied only by a distribution in which Alpha and Beta acquire equally large plots of land.

One might argue, on behalf of the 'equal-increment-of-increase' reading, that neither person has a greater claim on the island's unowned resources than the other. In so far as they have any claim at all, they have an equal claim. But if each person has an equal claim on the island's unowned resources, then one person would not be entitled to acquire the entire island, leaving the other with nothing. This would not be consistent with *an equal claim on the world's resources* as

Subjectivism, and Equal Opportunity for Welfare', *Philosophy and Public Affairs*, 19 (1990): 158–94. In Chapter 5 below I will defend such a preference-based measure of welfare on the grounds that it provides an acceptably neutral standard of welfare in the face of a diverse and often conflicting plurality of particular conceptions of the good.

[44] By a 'legitimate complaint' I mean one that is not overridden by countervailing considerations.

[45] Note that the two interpretations of 'to the same degree' yield the same result whenever individuals enjoy the same absolute level of welfare in the absence of any worldly resources. In actual fact, this would be the case, since, given our high degree of dependence on worldly resources for our survival and flourishing, each of us would enjoy roughly the same extremely low level of welfare in the absence of access to any worldly resources whatsoever.

opposed to *a claim to end up equally well off as others as the result of one's acquisition of resources.* When 'equal' modifies one's claim over the world's resources, then it makes sense to call for a distribution of shares of the world's resources that are of equal value in terms of opportunity of welfare for each—i.e. it makes sense to adopt the 'equal-increment-of-increase' reading.

I reject this argument because I reject the proposition that each person has an equal claim on the island's resources. I would maintain that, *ceteris paribus*, someone who would, through no fault of his on account of his mental and physical constitution, be worse off in terms of welfare than another under an equal distribution of resources has a greater claim on the island's resources than another who would be better off than he in terms of welfare. For to insist that such individuals have an equal claim is to commit oneself to the unfairness of a principle of acquisition which preserves disparities in the absolute levels of welfare of individuals caused by differences in their mental and physical constitution that are traceable to luck. Only a distribution that accords with the 'equal-absolute-level' reading would eliminate this unfairness. It follows from such a commitment to fairness that Alpha has a greater claim on the island's resources than Beta. I believe that Beta in fact has no legitimate claim on the island's resources, whereas Alpha has a legitimate claim to all of the island's resources.[46] This is because any claim to resources on Beta's part would presuppose that Beta is entitled, on account of the luck of his mental and physical constitution, to improve his lot through the acquisition of unowned resources at the expense of Alpha, who would thereby be consigned to a fate worse than Beta's would have been even in the absence of any resources. Such a claim could not be justified, and therefore Beta would have no legitimate complaint if Alpha were to acquire all of the island's resources.[47]

IV

I now turn to the task of reconciling libertarian self-ownership with an equality of the sort that is called for by the egalitarian proviso under

---

[46] This belief provides me with further reason to formulate the egalitarian proviso as entitling to an 'equally advantageous share' rather than an 'equal share', since an entitlement to an 'equal share' is inconsistent with this belief. (See n. 36 above.)

[47] It follows from my demonstration of the compatibility of self-ownership and equality in the next section that Beta's self-ownership would not be infringed if Alpha were to acquire all of the island's resources.

the welfarist specification that I have just offered. Cohen would argue that the affirmation of the egalitarian proviso implies the denial that we have a libertarian right of self-ownership, since he claims:

> An egalitarian might reject initial resource equality [i.e. a distribution of bundles of resources such that no one would want to swap his bundle with anybody else's] on the ground that resources need to be differentially distributed to compensate for talent differences. But that ground of rejection of resource equality requires denial of the tenet, derived from the [claim that we have a right] of self-ownership, that people are entitled to the differential rewards which (uncompensated for) talent differences produce.[48]

Contrary to Cohen, I do not believe that the aforementioned tenet can be derived from a libertarian right of self-ownership, since, as Cohen notes elsewhere, 'the principle of self-ownership . . . says, on the face of it, nothing about anyone's rights in resources other than people, and, in particular, nothing about the substances and capacities of nature, without which the things that people want cannot be produced'.[49] More precisely, libertarian self-ownership says nothing about rights in worldly resources beyond those that one is able to acquire through the exchange of one's labour (or parts of one's body) for goods that others are entitled to trade. It crucially does not have implications regarding the background of acquisition and distribution of worldly resources that provides the context for such exchanges. The recognition of a libertarian right of self-ownership does not rule out a distribution of resources in accordance with the egalitarian proviso any more than it rules out a distribution of worldly resources in accordance with a principle of joint ownership of the world that renders this right virtually worthless.[50] Cohen might argue that my *grounds* for affirming the egalitarian proviso, unlike the grounds that he has hypothesized for a right of joint ownership, imply the denial of a libertarian right of self-ownership. Nothing I say, however, implies that I deny the existence of either of the two rights that together constitute a libertarian right of self-ownership.[51] Consider the case of a

---

[48] Cohen, *Self-Ownership*, 162 n. 31.

[49] Ibid. 13.

[50] Cohen has famously argued that joint ownership of natural resources—whereby any use or consumption of the island's resources by one requires the consent of all—is consistent with uninfringed libertarian rights of self-ownership (ibid. chs. 3–4). Moreover, by neutralizing the bargaining advantage of the talented, such 'joint ownership prevents self-ownership from generating an inequality to which egalitarians would object' (ibid. 96). In circumstances of joint ownership, libertarian self-ownership would, however, be rendered virtually worthless, since one would be permitted to consume any bit of food or water or move, stand, or rest on any bit of land only with the collective permission of all (ibid. 97–9). Cf. Locke's attack on joint ownership in II. 28–9.

[51] I list these rights in Sect. I above.

land-reform policy that is relevantly analogous to the egalitarian proviso. Under this policy, ownership of government land is transferred
to individuals in inverse proportion to the value (measured in terms of
the opportunity for welfare that it provides) of the land that they have
already inherited from their ancestors so that the welfare that each can
derive from the sum total of her holdings in land after this transfer is
equal. Just as the egalitarian proviso compensates people for differences in their mental and physical capacities that bear on their effi-
ciency in converting resources into welfare, this policy compensates
people for differences in the value (in terms of welfare) of their initial
holdings in land. Yet the land-reform policy does not come into conflict with the claim that people had and continue to have equally
strong ownership rights over the initial holdings that they had inherited, where these rights include rights analogous to each of the two
rights that together constitute a libertarian right of self-ownership.
Their rights of control over and use of this inherited land are no less
strong than they were before the transfer of government land. Their
right to whatever income they could gain from this inherited land,
either through unregulated and untaxed trading or simply through
labouring upon the land without trading, is also unchanged by the
transfer of government land. The state would, no doubt, infringe a libertarian right of ownership over inherited land if, instead of pursuing
the above policy, it seized some of that land and transferred it to the
less well off or forced individuals to give the less well off half of whatever they gain through unregulated and untaxed exchanges. But it does
not infringe any libertarian right of ownership over land by giving
more land to those who have less and less to those who have more.
Similarly, the state does not infringe any libertarian right of ownership
over self by allowing those who have lesser talents to acquire more
land than those who have greater talents.

Even though the egalitarian proviso is, as I have just shown, consistent with an uninfringed libertarian right of self-ownership, it places
no constraints upon the achievement of equality of opportunity for
welfare by means of a distribution of worldly resources that leaves the
able-bodied with so few resources that they would be forced, on pain
of starvation, to come to the assistance of the less talented. Imagine an
island whose inhabitants consist of one able-bodied woman named
Able and one man named Unable who is incapable of engaging in any
productive labour whatsoever. Able is a non-altruistic ascetic who has
no desire for any land or other material goods beyond that which is
sufficient for her survival. In these circumstances, the only division of
worldly resources (consistent with libertarian self-ownership and the

survival of each) that would give rise to equality of opportunity for welfare is one in which Unable is entitled to acquire so much of the island that Able would be left with a sliver of land that is insufficient for her to draw the sustenance necessary for her survival. Given such a distribution, Unable would have the power to exclude Able from land that is essential to her sustenance and would therefore have the power to force Able to work for him for the rest of his life by granting her permission to work his land on the condition that she share a portion of the fruits of her labour on his land with him. Since the two parties would have equal bargaining power under such a distribution, and assuming that they are purely rationally self-interested, it is reasonable to infer that Unable would settle for no less than an arrangement in which Able must work for his sake for the rest of their lives, and that Able would agree to such an arrangement, but only under conditions that ensure their equality of opportunity for welfare.[52] Able's predicament is consistent with her possession of an uninfringed libertarian right of self-ownership. But, as in the case of joint ownership, such a right would not be worth very much to her, since she would not have rights over a sufficient amount of worldly resources to provide any buffer against her being forced to work for the sake of Unable.

I shall define a libertarian right of self-ownership as 'robust' if and only if, in addition to having the libertarian right itself, one also has rights over enough worldly resources to ensure that one will not be forced by necessity to come to the assistance of others in a manner involving the sacrifice of one's life, limb, or labour. If it could be shown that the egalitarian proviso could be rendered consistent with a libertarian right of self-ownership only when the able-bodied are deprived of so many resources that their right is not robust and they are forced, on pain of starvation, to work for the disabled, then one will have achieved nothing more than a Pyrrhic reconciliation of self-ownership and equality. The task of reconciliation is to show that egalitarianism is consistent not merely with an uninfringed libertarian right of self-ownership, but with such a right that is, moreover, *robust*.

As the story of Able and Unable illustrates, if the able-bodied have no desire for resources beyond that which is necessary for subsistence, equality can be achieved only if the able-bodied are entitled to acquire so few worldly resources that their libertarian right of self-ownership is not robust. That having been said, I would like to offer my promised

---

[52] See John Roemer, *Theories of Distributive Justice* (Cambridge, Mass.: Harvard University Press, 1996), 211–12.

demonstration of how a robust-libertarian right of self-ownership for all could as a matter of contingent fact be reconciled with equality if we assume more ordinary preferences for material resources among the able-bodied. The libertarian's critique of egalitarianism is enfeebled in the following manner. When, as is typically the case, the able-bodied have a preference for material goods in excess of that which is necessary for their subsistence, it would in principle (i.e. leaving aside problems of institutional or political infeasibility) be possible to provide a fairly wide range of disabled members of society with the opportunity to acquire enough worldly resources to generate a steady, generous, and lifelong flow of income from the investment, rental, or sale of these resources. Such income would enable these disabled individuals to better themselves to the same degree as able-bodied individuals who are themselves provided with the opportunity to acquire a fairly generous portion of worldly resources. The holdings of the able-bodied would be sufficiently generous that the disabled would be able to support themselves through truly voluntary exchanges with the able-bodied that did not involve forced assistance. By these means, one could achieve equality without any encroachments upon any robust-libertarian right of self-ownership. To provide a simple and artificial illustration of such an arrangement, imagine an island society divided into a large number of able-bodied and a smaller number of disabled individuals. All the sea-front property is divided among the disabled, and farmable land in the interior is divided among the able-bodied. The able-bodied each voluntarily purchase access to the beach in exchange for the provision of food to the disabled. The result of this division of land is that the disabled and the able-bodied are each able to better themselves to an equal degree without anyone's being forced to come to the assistance of anybody else.[53] The bounty of worldly

---

[53] Frances Kamm has suggested that libertarians and other deontologists could object that the able-bodied are used as means in the following respect in this scenario. The distribution of resources that the egalitarian proviso mandates is specifically designed to achieve equality of welfare by inducing the able-bodied to enter into labour (and other) contracts with the disabled that they would not choose to enter into if resources had instead been divided equally (i.e. into shares of equal market value). Yet even if this amounts to a using of the able-bodied as means, I do not regard this as an objectionable use, since the means employed in this case are non-coercive and do not deprive the able-bodied of anything to which they have even a prima-facie entitlement. This arrangement involves no more objectionable a using of persons as means than Rawls's difference principle, which gives the able-bodied a greater than equal division of resources in order to induce them to produce more than they otherwise would when this would benefit the badly off (see Rawls, ibid. 75–83, 150–1). Of course, Rawls's difference principle gives the able-bodied more than they would have had under an equal division of resources, whereas the egalitarian proviso gives them less. Therefore, the able-bodied would (in so far as they are self-interested) prefer Rawls's difference principle to an equal division, whereas they would prefer an equal division to the distribution called for by the egalitarian proviso. But this fact would provide the

resources and the preferences and number of the able-bodied that typ-
ify more realistically large and heterogeneous societies would ensure
that land and other worldly resources can in principle be divided in a
manner that allows a fairly wide range of the disabled—including
some of those who are completely incapable of farming, harvesting, or
gathering any food from the land—to better themselves from their
holdings of worldly resources to the same degree as the able-bodied
without forcing the able-bodied to come to their assistance. It is, for
example, difficult to see what would in principle rule out the redistribution of land and other worldly resources to a fairly wide range of the
disabled in a relatively prosperous society such as the United States so
that they would have enough capital with which to purchase the goods
of life through voluntary exchanges with able-bodied individuals.[54]

We are now in a position to see why the following assertion of
Cohen's is misleading (even if not, strictly speaking, false):

[N]o egalitarian rule regarding external resources alone will, together with
self-ownership, deliver equality of outcome, except, as in the case of joint
ownership, at an unacceptable sacrifice of autonomy [i.e. the circumstances of
genuine control over one's life]. There is a tendency of self-ownership to produce inequality, and the only way to nullify that tendency (without expressly
abridging self-ownership) is through a regime over external resources which
is so rigid that it excludes exercise of independent rights over oneself.[55]

able-bodied with grounds for complaint against the egalitarian proviso only if there were an initial moral presumption in favour of an equal division of resources. I deny any such presumption.

   [54] In ordinary circumstances it would, however, be impossible to equalize the opportunity for
welfare of some disabled individuals without forcing others to come to their assistance. For some
such individuals the resources required to raise their level of welfare would be so fantastically
great (e.g. the spending of the enormous amounts of money that would be necessary and sufficient to find the cure for certain debilitating diseases) that people would have to be forced to
labour on their behalf in order to generate the resources. Andrew Williams notes that there may
be other ordinary circumstances in which no amount of natural resources (consistent with the
robust self-ownership of others) could compensate somebody for a disability, yet a forced transfer of body parts could. (A totally blind person who could have her vision partially restored only
through the transplantation of an eye from a fully sighted two-eyed person might be in such a
situation.) In written comments John Roemer has calculated that, given what he regards as the
realistic assumption that labour is ten times more important to production than natural
resources, and if we also assume that the disabled need to consume four times as many resources
as the able-bodied to achieve a given increase in the level of welfare, it will be possible to reconcile equality with robust self-ownership by the means that I have proposed so long as the disabled constitute less than 5.5 per cent of the population. If natural resources are more important
to production relative to labour, or if the difference in the rate of conversion of resources into
welfare of the able-bodied versus the disabled is smaller, then it will be possible to reconcile
robust self-ownership with equality even if the disabled constitute a larger percentage of the population.

   [55] Cohen, *Self-Ownership*, 105.

This statement is misleading because it fails to acknowledge that, as a contingent fact, it will be possible, across a fairly wide range of individuals, to nullify the tendency of an uninfringed and robust-libertarian right of self-ownership to produce inequality. As sketched in the previous paragraph, such a nullification would be achieved by means of a distribution of worldly resources that is in accordance with the egalitarian proviso. In a society in which resources are so distrib-uted, the munificently endowed disabled could justify their equality of opportunity for welfare not on the grounds of a positive right to demand that unwilling others come to their assistance by sharing the hard-earned fruits of their labour, but rather on the grounds that they have a right to a share of worldly resources that enables them to secure the same level of advantage as anybody else. They would not, there-fore, need to respond to any charges of parasitism or free riding,[56] since their case for equality of opportunity for welfare would rest on nothing more than the staking of a claim to a fair share of worldly resources to which nobody else has a prior or stronger moral claim. Libertarians such as Nozick have sought to build their political philo-sophy on high moral ground—that of a stringent libertarian right of self-ownership that is supposed to reflect our elevated status as invio-lable persons. The purpose of this chapter has been to show that egalitarians can build there too. The Lockean egalitarianism I have sketched is, indeed, far more deferential to the preservation of a *robust*-libertarian right of self-ownership than Nozick's libertarian-ism, since the inegalitarian proviso of the latter provides very little protection against the forced labour of the propertyless.

V

So far I have, for the sake of simplicity, restricted myself to a highly schematized model of a single generation of strangers on an island in order to make a case for the egalitarian proviso. Even if one accepts the egalitarian proviso as a valid principle of justice in acquisition of unowned worldly resources in this context, one might wonder what relevance it has to the question of justice in holdings in the real world in which there are now very few worldly resources left to discover and there have been and will continue to be multiple generations of inhab-itants. It is no doubt true that nearly every bit of the world has some

---

[56] David Gauthier has levelled these two charges against egalitarianism (see Gauthier, *Morals by Agreement* (Oxford: Oxford University Press, 1986), 217–21).

legal claim of ownership attached to it today. But it does not follow
that the egalitarian proviso is irrelevant to the question of the distribution of resources at the present day. It is relevant because, as I will
argue, the egalitarian proviso, when fully spelled out, requires that the
members of each succeeding generation have at least as great an opportunity to own worldly resources as did the first generation to acquire
resources out of a state of nature.[57]

Let us assume, again for the sake of simplicity, that generations are
discrete collections of equal numbers of individuals of the same age,
that a new generation comes into adulthood only after the old generation has passed away, and that the composition of future generations
does not depend on the decisions of past generations. Under these
conditions, a reasonable interpretation of the egalitarian proviso
would place some limitations on what one is entitled to do at the time
of one's death with that which one has acquired. Assume, as a *reductio
ad absurdum*, that the egalitarian proviso calls for acquisitions that
preserve equality of ability to better oneself among only members of
one's own generation; yet it sanctions rights of ownership over
worldly resources that include the right to consume or destroy that
which one owns. It would follow that the first generation to confront
unowned resources would be permitted by the egalitarian proviso to
divide all worldly resources among themselves and bleed dry and then
scorch the earth at the end of their lives, thereby rendering it worthless for all subsequent generations. Such an interpretation of the
egalitarian proviso would introduce an arbitrary and indefensible bias
against future generations. Problems of a similar nature would arise if
one were to allow rights to bequeath one's holdings to whomever one
chooses. If the egalitarian proviso were to sanction bequests of one's
entire holdings to whomever one chooses, then the members of the
first generation could divide all worldly resources among themselves
and then bequeath all of their holdings to a very few, leaving the
majority of the next generation landless paupers. Again, the unlucky
many among subsequent generations could complain that the proviso
is arbitrarily and indefensibly biased against them.

One could eliminate these biases by modifying the egalitarian proviso so that it instead demands acquisitions that leave enough for the
members of *all* generations to better themselves to the same degree.
But if people were still to retain, and regularly to exercise, a right completely to consume, destroy, or bequeath to whomever they choose

---

[57] Here I assume 'other things being equal'—e.g. that the size of each generation remains the
same and that the stock of worldly resources is not depleted by natural events.

whatever they have acquired out of a state of nature, then we would be faced with a new and only slightly less embarrassing difficulty: rights of acquisition would need to be severely limited in the face of multiple generations. In order to guarantee such intergenerational equality of ability to better oneself, and still assuming that generations are of the same size, each individual would need to be restricted so that she has the right to acquire no more than roughly one-nth of the island, where n is the total number of individuals who will ever inhabit this island.[58] If we assume a very large number of generations, then each individual would be entitled to acquire only a minute sliver. (If we assume an infinite number of generations, then nobody would be entitled to more than an infinitesimally small sliver.) In the light of these difficulties, it is reasonable to deny the existence of complete rights to consume, destroy, or bequeath those resources that one has acquired from an unowned state. It would make far more sense to insist that the members of each generation ensure that, at their deaths, resources that are at least as valuable as those that they have acquired lapse back into a state of non-ownership. Each succeeding generation would therefore face anew a world of unowned resources that is undiminished when compared with that which faced the previous generation. The members of each generation would therefore have the same opportunity as their predecessors to acquire resources from an unowned state.

For all I have said, the members of one generation could, through labour, investment, or technological innovation, greatly increase the total value of their holdings so that a surplus of wealth would remain even after they have ensured that, at their deaths, resources that are at least as valuable as those that they have acquired lapse back into a state of non-ownership. Imagine that a number of equally talented individuals find themselves on a previously undiscovered and forested island. In accordance with the egalitarian proviso, they divide the island into equal-sized plots. Some harvest the timber from their justly acquired portions of the island to build yachts. Thereafter they plant additional trees to ensure that the plots of land that will lapse into non-ownership at their deaths are just as good as the ones that they first acquired. The others, who are less industrious, simply gather nuts and berries by day and sleep under the stars at night. Would the egalitarian proviso allow members of the first generation to bequeath their yachts to whomever among the members of the second generation they choose? On a plausible interpretation of the proviso, such bequests

---

[58] Here I assume, for simplicity, that each is roughly equally efficient as a producer, consumer, and trader at converting resources into welfare. Similar difficulties will arise even if people are highly unequally efficient in these regards.

would be ruled out for the following reason. Since individuals possess only a lifetime leasehold on worldly resources, they have nothing more than a lifetime leasehold on whatever worldly resources they improve. They should be forewarned that any worldly object they improve through their labour will lapse into a state of non-ownership upon their death and hence will not be bequeathable. Individuals have nothing more than a lifetime leasehold on the timber that they transform into yachts and hence nothing more than a lifetime leasehold on the yachts.[59]

Even if bequests are ruled out on the above grounds, this discussion raises the more general question of the compatibility of any strongly egalitarian principle of distribution with either of the following two rights: (1) the right to engage in the non-market transfers of worldly resources in the form of intragenerational gifts or (2) the right to engage in the non-market pooling and sharing of worldly resources (as occurs, for example, in marriages). There would be little reason from an egalitarian point of view to interfere with the worthwhile practices of modest gift giving on special occasions which do not, in the aggregate, have a significant affect on the distribution of opportunity for welfare. But an egalitarian will need to prohibit or regulate—or else compensate non-beneficiaries in order to counteract—less modest transfers or sharings which would otherwise significantly disrupt equality of opportunity for welfare.

At least in the case of resources which are the product of one's labour, one might object that such measures would constitute a violation of the rights of self-ownership of those who would like to transfer or share their resources. Such an objection would rest on the claim that the two rights listed in the previous paragraph are corollaries of the second of the two rights of libertarian self-ownership, which is the right to all of the income one can gain from one's mind and body, including one's labour. One might argue that one doesn't really have a right to all of the income one can gain from one's labour if one doesn't have the right to spend this income on others as well as oneself during one's lifetime. In the case of someone who would like to spend his income on others, his income is worth less to him if he is not allowed to do so than it would have been if he had been allowed to do so. For any amount of income x none of which one can spend on others, those who would like to spend some of their income on others will typically be indifferent between possessing that amount x and possessing some

---

[59] Ross Harrison has drawn an analogy to what happens to improvements you make to an apartment on which you have a leasehold rather than a freehold. You lose your ownership of the paint that you applied to the walls of your flat when your leasehold runs out.

lesser amount $x-y$ which they may spend on others as well as themselves. Prohibiting one from spending one's income x on others might therefore be regarded as the equivalent of a confiscatory tax of the amount y.

This argument is plausible when applied to cases in which one's income is not generated through any interaction with the world. Recall the case discussed earlier of the individual whose income consists of the articles of clothing she weaves out of her own hair. Her being forbidden to give this clothing away to others might plausibly be regarded as a diminution of her right of self-ownership. And it might be equated with the partial confiscation of a wardrobe which she is entitled to give away. But this argument does not establish a right to give away one's income to whomever one pleases when this income has been generated through labour which involves the world as well as oneself. To see why it does not, consider the following variation of a case presented earlier. Suppose that a farmer's income consists of the crops that he harvests from the land that he farms. If he came rightfully to own this land by purchasing it on condition that he not give away any of his harvest, then it would not be any violation of his right of self-ownership if he were prevented from doing so in order to enforce the terms of his purchase. By parity of reasoning, a person's self-ownership would not be violated when he is constrained by the egalitarian proviso from engaging in the non-market transfer of income generated through interaction with the world. In this case as well as the previous one, a person's right of ownership over worldly resources does not extend to the right to give away income generated through interaction with these worldly resources. Hence, preventing someone from transferring these resources is a means of preventing him from doing things with the world that he has no right to do, rather than an infringement of his right of self-ownership.

VI

I would like to conclude with some remarks on the practical relevance of my reconciliation of self-ownership and equality. It would be difficult to know, at the outset of any given generation, what division of resources would guarantee equality of opportunity for welfare among individuals whose robust-libertarian self-ownership is respected and hence what division of resources would satisfy the egalitarian proviso. Hence, any initial distribution of property rights would be provisional and subject to revision. The state would need to engage in *ex post facto* adjustments to people's initial shares in order to achieve equality. It would not be proper for the State to level differences that arise from choices for which individuals can be held morally responsible so long as these choices are made against a background of property rights that ensure equality of opportunity for welfare. But it would be necessary for it to engage in relatively frequent redistribution in order to ensure that such a background exists and persists. It would be a mistake to regard these interventions as objectionable on the grounds that they constitute violations or infringements of the property rights of individuals, since they are instead a necessary means of realizing a just distribution of worldly resources in accordance with the principle of justice in acquisition. Such an adjustment would be no more a violation or even an infringement of somebody's property rights than the taking of someone's holdings in order to rectify the fact that these holdings were unjustly passed down to him.[60] One might nevertheless object that the institutions and practices that would be necessary to gather the relevant information and make the relevant adjustments would either be practically impossible or too costly in terms both of the funding they would require and of their intrusive effects on the lives of individuals. Nothing I have said in this chapter can lay to rest these practical difficulties with egalitarianism. Rather, I have been concerned to address a problem of a different sort: the putative conflict between self-ownership and equality at the level of ideal theory. My main aim has been to refute one prominent philosophical argument for the claim that the complete realization of equality would be unattractive even in the absence of these practical difficulties. I believe that the most serious objections to egalitarianism are practical not principled. There are already enough problems in the world. Philosophers should not add to the mess.

---

[60] Nozick himself is rightly sensitive to the grounds that one offers for redistribution. He believes that an egalitarian pattern of distribution can be imposed if and only if it is necessary to rectify past injustices (see Nozick, *Anarchy*, 230–1).

CHAPTER 2

Making the Unjust Provide for the Disabled

I have argued in Chapter 1 that it is possible, across a fairly wide range of individuals who differ in their capacity to derive welfare from resources, to distribute initially unowned worldly resources so as to achieve equality of opportunity for welfare in a manner which is compatible with each person's possession of an uninfringed libertarian right of self-ownership that is robust rather than merely formal. It is possible to provide a fairly wide range of disabled members of society with the opportunity to acquire enough worldly resources to better themselves, via the investment, rental, or sale of these resources, to the same degree as able-bodied individuals who are themselves provided with the opportunity to acquire a fairly generous portion of worldly resources. The holdings of the able-bodied would be sufficiently generous that the disabled would be able to support themselves through truly voluntary exchanges with the able-bodied that do not involve forced assistance. By these means, one could achieve equality of opportunity for welfare across this range of individuals without any encroachments upon anyone's robust-libertarian right of self-ownership.

In this chapter I would like to address the question of what, if anything, is to be done when it is possible to provide for the basic needs of some individuals only through a distribution of resources which encroaches upon the robust-libertarian rights of self-ownership of others. Let us suppose that a given segment of the population are disabled in the following respect: through no fault of theirs, they lack the ability to engage in productive labour. Suppose that, in the absence of voluntary charitable contributions, their basic needs for food, clothing, shelter, and medicine will be met only if others who are able-bodied are forced to engage in productive labour on their behalf.[1] Moreover, we shall assume that the rest of the population are able to engage in productive labour yet lack the desire to engage in any productive labour beyond that which is necessary for their own subsistence. If the rights of self-ownership of these able-bodied individuals are to be robust, then they must own enough worldly resources to sustain themselves. But if they have enough to sustain themselves, they will have no motive to engage in any labour which would sustain the disabled, no matter how wealthy the latter may be. Let us assume that each of the able-bodied owns enough farmable land to sustain himself. He also owns enough farmable land to sustain others if he so chooses, yet he lets this land remain fallow, given his lack of motivation to provide for more than his own subsistence.

I would like to propose that liberal egalitarians who endorse the welfare state and libertarians who endorse the minimal state can find common ground in support of an unfamiliar means of forcing able-bodied individuals to come to the assistance of the disabled in order to provide for their basic needs.[2] Such means would not, as is typically the case, involve the redistributive taxation of the income of able-bodied individuals across the board, where this tax is ultimately enforced by coercive threat of imprisonment. Rather, assistance to the disabled would be provided by the coercive taxation of only those able-bodied individuals who have been properly convicted of performing justifiably criminalized acts. I will refer to such convicts as 'the unjust'.[3]

In Section I I will argue that many liberal egalitarians will discover that a strong case can be made for the taxation of the unjust, since such a scheme would mitigate the objectionable nature of the coercion that must be applied in order to provide for the disabled, even if this case is ultimately less strong than the case that can be made for the coercive taxation of all able-bodied individuals. In Section II I will argue that libertarians who reject standard schemes of coercive redistributive tax-

---

[1] Here the focus shifts from equality of opportunity for welfare to basic needs, for the following reason. As I argued in Chapter 1 Sections I–II above, forcing people to engage in productive labour merely to provide for the basic needs of others is much less difficult to defend than forcing people to engage in productive labour to provide for others all the way to the point of equality where inequalities would persist even after the basic needs of each have been met.

[2] John Rawls's *A Theory of Justice* (Cambridge, Mass.: Harvard University Press, 1971) and Ronald Dworkin's *Sovereign Virtue* (Cambridge, Mass.: Harvard University Press, 2000) provide paradigm cases of the sort of liberal egalitarianism under discussion, whereas Robert Nozick's *Anarchy, State, and Utopia* (New York: Basic Books, 1974) provides a paradigm case of the sort of libertarianism under discussion.

[3] I adopt this name simply as a convenient and reasonably descriptive shorthand. I do not thereby commit myself to the claim that all injustices, or that only injustices, should be criminal offences.

ation will not also be able to resist the case for taxation of the unjust. In Section III I will defend taxation of the unjust against the objection that it would call for punishment in excess of what justice permits.

In making these arguments I will consider the following four methods of raising revenue which would be sufficient to sustain the disabled: (1) involuntary, inescapable, and coercively enforced taxation of the able-bodied that ensures that each of them makes a roughly equal sacrifice on behalf of the disabled (*universal taxation*);[4] (2) voluntary contributions by each able-bodied individual, where the contributions are identical to the amount they would have been taxed under the previous scenario (*universal giving*); (3) voluntary contributions exclusively from a very generous but relatively small portion of those who are able-bodied (*non-universal giving*); or (4) coercive taxation of only those amongst the able-bodied who have been properly convicted of performing justifiably criminalized acts that it was reasonable to expect them to avoid committing, and which they committed even though they knew that they would be subject to such taxation for doing so (*taxation of the unjust*).

I

I hope to convince liberal egalitarians that, unlike the extreme-libertarian minimal state in which the disabled are allowed to starve when charity is not forthcoming, taxation of the unjust is reasonably just, even if not as just as universal taxation. My argument for the claim that liberal egalitarians ought to find a reasonably strong case for taxation of the unjust will unfold as follows.

P1 Liberal egalitarians should regard the case for non-universal giving as at least as strong as the case for universal taxation.

P2 Taxation of the unjust, while not as good as non-universal giving, shares many of the most important virtues of non-universal giving.

Therefore, liberal egalitarians should regard the case for taxation of the unjust as reasonably strong, even if not as strong as the case for universal taxation.

---

[4] This might take the form of a lump-sum tax on each of the able-bodied which would generate enough revenue to sustain each of the disabled.

A Defence of P1

Liberal egalitarians would agree that universal giving is the best of the four alternatives that I have sketched above, since each citizen would voluntarily make a roughly equal sacrifice in sustaining the disabled. Liberal egalitarians would approve of both the voluntariness and the universal and egalitarian nature of the giving. They would thus prefer universal giving to non-universal giving, since the latter would lack the universal and egalitarian features of the former and all else would be equal. They would presumably also prefer universal giving to taxation of the unjust, since the latter, in addition to lacking the universal and egalitarian features of the former, would also involve the coercion of those who have committed injustices. Moreover, it seems clear that liberal egalitarians would prefer universal giving to universal taxation since the two alternatives would be equally attractive save for the fact that universal taxation involves coercion, and universal giving does not.

But what are the relative merits, in the eyes of a liberal egalitarian, of universal taxation versus non-universal giving? Unlike libertarians such as Nozick, liberal egalitarians would have no objection to universal taxation if it were the only way to provide for the disabled. But suppose that liberal egalitarians were presented with the following choice between universal taxation and non-universal giving. Suppose that one day they awaken to the startling news that a minority of the population has volunteered to give in a manner that fully provides for the disabled. Would liberal egalitarians prefer universal taxation to such non-universal giving? Being egalitarians, they would claim that, in one important respect, universal taxation is superior to non-universal giving, since in the case of universal taxation each person makes a roughly equal sacrifice in providing for the disabled. But, being liberals, they would claim that, in another important respect, non-universal giving is superior to universal taxation, since in the case of non-universal giving assistance to the disabled is provided without recourse to inescapable state coercion. I believe that many liberal egalitarians would place more weight on the avoidance of coercion than the realization of an egalitarian distribution of the cost of providing for the disabled. These liberal egalitarians would therefore conclude that, all things considered, non-universal giving is to be preferred to universal taxation.

If, for example, liberal egalitarians knew that enough money fully to provide for the disabled had been voluntarily raised and donated to the state by a small portion of the population, I doubt that many would insist that the state go ahead and coercively tax the non-generous majority of the population and give the generous minority partial rebates to ensure that each citizen make an equal sacrifice. In fact, many liberal egalitarians already prefer voluntary schemes to universal and egalitarian involuntary schemes in the case of national defence. Many believe, for example, that, so long as it is possible to raise an army for the national defence through volunteers, the state should rely on volunteers rather than conscript from the general population. They favour an all-volunteer army over the imposition of an equal actual burden (the conscription of each for short stints) or an equal and by no means trivial expected burden (the conscription via a fair lottery of only some for longer stints) on the entire population of able-bodied individuals.

In order to forestall a possible objection to non-universal giving, I should note that it would be a mistake for liberal egalitarians to argue that they would have reason to prefer universal taxation to non-universal giving on the grounds that the former, but not the latter, provides a legal guarantee of assistance to the disabled. This would be a mistake because non-universal giving does not preclude the state from offering the following guarantee to the disabled: that coercive taxes would be imposed to raise the necessary revenue to meet their needs if voluntary contributions should prove insufficient. Such a guarantee is consistent with freedom from coercion or fear of coercion so long as the likelihood of the imposition of coercive taxes is sufficiently low. To illustrate this point by means of analogy: The all-volunteer army is backed up by the certainty of a draft in the event that there are not enough volunteers to meet vital defence needs. But if the likelihood of a draft is sufficiently low, then such a back-up plan is in practice consistent with freedom from conscription or fear of conscription.

Some liberal egalitarians will nevertheless object to non-universal giving on the different grounds that it permits able-bodied individuals to shirk their obligation to give to the disabled. But what are the grounds for affirming such an obligation? Why doesn't one have an obligation to give to those who are disabled only if there are such people who stand in need of assistance? Under a scheme of non-universal giving there would be no such people, since the generous minority would already have provided for their needs.

The non-contributing majority could not convincingly be accused of violating an obligation to refrain from 'free riding'. This is because the benefit of redistribution to the disabled is not, except perhaps in some minor respects, a 'public good' that the non-generous majority cannot be excluded from receiving even though they do not contribute towards its realization. Redistribution is, for the most part, a non-public good that is exclusively directed toward the disabled rather than a good that is enjoyed by the non-generous majority. It is a public good only in the very limited respect that providing for the disabled allows all to enjoy the benefit of living in a society that is less indecent than it would have been if the disabled were allowed to starve. But the benefit that each able-bodied person receives from the creation of a welfare state would not be likely to outweigh the cost to him of contribution toward the welfare state under universal taxation. Thus it is unlikely that the 'principle of fairness' would generate any obligation to contribute toward the realization of a welfare state.[5]

Perhaps the objection to non-universal giving proceeds from the observation that the able-bodied each stand in the same special relation to those who happen to be amongst the disabled. This relation is that of being members of the same society as they, and such shared membership might be thought to ground an equal obligation on the part of each of the able-bodied to provide for the disabled. This obligation might be regarded as non-transferable in so far as it cannot be discharged by one person on behalf of another. The following analogy to the special relation in which children stand to their parents might be invoked in support of these claims. Siblings are typically obliged to make an equal sacrifice in order to ensure that their parents are provided for in their old age. They would shirk their duties if they were to allow a single one of them voluntarily to cover the entire cost of such provision. But one can take the analogy to the family only so far. In the first place, the equal obligation of children to assist their parents is typically grounded in the fact that their parents have impartially benefited each of them. But such considerations of reciprocity and gratitude do not play much of a role in grounding obligations to the disabled in a society. Second, unlike the typical parent–child relation, the relation between the able-bodied and the disabled in a society is almost entirely a relation amongst strangers and hence a rather thin and impersonal one on which to base a non-transferable obligation of each of the able-bodied to provide for the disabled.

---

[5] One could more readily appeal to the principle of fairness in order to justify universal taxation for the purpose of providing police protection and national defence, since in these cases those who fail to contribute under a voluntary scheme would receive a substantial benefit for free from a public good that was created by the joint sacrifices of others. For a discussion of the principle of fairness see George Klosko, *The Principle of Fairness and Political Obligation* (Lanham: Rowman & Littlefield, 1992).

A Defence of P2

I now turn to the second premiss of my argument that liberal egalitarians should be sympathetic to the taxation of the unjust. This premiss states that taxation of the unjust, while not as good as non-universal giving, shares many of the most important virtues of the latter alternative.

Taxation of the unjust is clearly less desirable than non-universal giving in so far as the proper motivation for parting with one's money is lacking on the part of the unjust. Revenue is coercively extracted via threat of imprisonment rather than voluntarily contributed for the sake of meeting the needs and entitlements of the disabled.[6] Moreover, in so far as the cost of aiding the disabled is unequally shared in the case of taxation of the unjust as well as non-universal giving but not in the case of universal taxation, universal taxation is superior from an egalitarian point of view to taxation of the unjust as well as non-universal giving.

There is, however, an important respect in which taxation of the unjust, like non-universal giving and unlike universal taxation, is a voluntary scheme and in this respect much to be preferred to universal taxation. In the case of taxation of the unjust as opposed to universal taxation, one's forced contribution is the consequence of an unforced choice to do wrong. More precisely, one is forced to make a contribution to the disabled only if one has voluntarily performed an illegal act that one had no right to perform and could reasonably have been expected to refrain from performing. The following remarks of H. L. A. Hart are relevant here:

[E]ach individual is given a *fair* opportunity to choose between keeping the law required for society's protection or paying the penalty . . . [Punishment] appears as a price justly extracted because the criminal had a fair opportunity beforehand to avoid liability to pay.

Criminal punishment . . . defers action till harm has been done; its primary operation consists simply in announcing certain standards of behaviour and attaching penalties for deviation, making it less eligible, and then leaving individuals to choose. This is a method of social control which maximizes individual freedom within the coercive framework of law in a number of different ways . . . First, the individual has an option between obeying or paying . . . Secondly, this system not only enables individuals to exercise this choice but increases the power of individuals to identify beforehand periods when the

---

[6] Note that the proper motivation to part with one's money is also lacking in the case of universal taxation when such taxes are forthcoming only because of the threat of imprisonment.

law's punishment will not interfere with them and to plan their lives accordingly.[7]

For some liberal egalitarians these sorts of considerations should be sufficient to tip the balance in favour of taxation of the unjust when compared with universal taxation.

Many liberal egalitarians regard standard schemes of redistributive universal taxation as justified because necessary to provide assistance for the disabled even though they regard the inescapable coercion of such schemes as bad. Before they entertained the possibility of a welfare state supported by taxation of the unjust, they might have believed that the badness of inescapable coercion was overridden by the justice of redistribution to the disabled that such universal taxation achieves. Once apprised of this possibility, however, they would have good reason to prefer taxation of the unjust to universal taxation, since the former takes most of the sting out of state coercion by exempting all who refrain from doing that which they have no right to do from such coercion. These liberal egalitarians might well prefer taxation of the unjust to universal taxation when sufficient revenue could be raised by means of taxation of the unjust, even though they would not reject universal taxation when sufficient revenues could not be raised through taxation of the unjust. Whether they would prefer taxation of the unjust to universal taxation when sufficient revenue could be raised would depend on how strongly they were bothered by the fact that taxation of the unjust results in an unequal sharing of the cost of aiding the disabled. But it is not likely that those who were strongly bothered by inescapable coercion would be even more strongly bothered by an unequal sharing of the cost of aiding the disabled, and the strongly bothered would therefore be likely to prefer taxation of the unjust to universal taxation.[8]

---

[7] H. L. A. Hart, 'Prolegomenon to the Principles of Punishment', in *Punishment and Responsibility* (Oxford: Oxford University Press, 1967), 22–3.

[8] Some liberal egalitarians might want to recommend the following alternative to taxation of the unjust as a means of avoiding the inescapable coercion of universal taxation: a redistributive tax that is imposed only on those who have reached a certain high level of income. They might argue that such a tax would share much of the voluntary nature of taxation of the unjust, since it would make the coercion escapable because it is conditional upon one's having earned a high income. Those who do not want to pay the tax can simply refrain from earning a high income. But what's wrong with this scheme is that it, unlike taxation of the unjust, penalizes those who choose to do something that they are entitled to do—earn a lot of money. Recall that the choice to earn a lot of money would be made against a fair background of a distribution of worldly resources that equalizes the opportunity for welfare of the able-bodied.

II

Having just argued that many liberal egalitarians should find a strong case for taxation of the unjust, even if not as strong as the case for universal taxation, I will now argue that the libertarian does not have good reason to prefer the minimal state to taxation of the unjust. Libertarians such as Nozick consider standard schemes of redistributive universal taxation to be unjustified because they regard the inescapable coercion of such schemes as a great evil. Such libertarians should, however, be able to endorse taxation of the unjust as a sufficiently voluntary means of raising revenue for assistance to the disabled when purely voluntary contributions are not forthcoming. If, for example, taxation of the unjust is to be regarded as a form of punishment, then a libertarian could not immediately object to it as a morally objectionable practice that is on a par with forced labour.[9] This is because libertarianism, unlike anarchism, affirms the justice of punishing those who violate the rights of others. Some theories of the justification of punishment might rule out punitive taxation of the unjust where 'punitive taxation of the unjust' refers to taxation of the unjust that is regarded as punishment. But libertarianism does not demand adherence to any such theory.

Nozick himself, for example, adheres to a retributivist theory of punishment that would condemn excess punitive taxation of the unjust, since his retributivism places upper limits on the severity of the punishments and fines that may be visited upon a criminal.[10] Nevertheless, he acknowledges the

interesting possibility that contemporary governments might make penalties (in addition to compensation [to the victims of crime]) monetary, and use them to finance various government activities. Perhaps some resources left to spend would be yielded by the retributive penalties in addition to compensation, and by the extra penalties needed to deter because of less than certain apprehension. Since the victims of the crimes of those people apprehended are fully compensated, it is not clear that the remaining funds . . . must go toward compensating the victims of uncaught criminals. Presumably a protective association would use such funds to reduce the price of its services.[11]

As far as I can tell, there is nothing in Nozick's libertarianism that would bar the state from using such leftover funds to provide

---

[9] Nozick raises this objection in *Anarchy, State, and Utopia*, 169–71. See Ch. 1 Sect. II above for a discussion of Nozick's objection.

[10] See Nozick, *Anarchy, State, and Utopia*, 59–63. See also Nozick, *Philosophical Explanations* (Cambridge, Mass.: Harvard University Press, 1981), 364, 371.

[11] Nozick, *Anarchy, State, and Utopia*, 62 n.

assistance to the disabled rather than a rebate to all taxpayers, and hence nothing in his libertarianism that would stand in the way of as much of a welfare state as could be provided by these leftover funds.

More generally, one can find, in Hart's writings on the rationale for excuses from punishment, the basis for a theory of punishment that is both congenial to the tenets of libertarianism and supportive of punitive taxation of the unjust. Hart remarks that

each individual person is to be protected against the claim of the rest for the highest possible measure of security, happiness or welfare which could be got at his expense by condemning him for a breach of the rules and punishing him. For this a moral licence is required in the form of proof that the person punished broke the law by an action which was the outcome of his free choice . . . Justice simply consists of principles to be observed in adjusting the competing claims of human beings which (i) treat all alike as persons by attaching special significance to human voluntary actions and (ii) forbid the use of one human being for the benefit of others except in return for his voluntary actions against them.[12]

On an account of punishment that draws its inspiration from these remarks, the punishment of individuals for the benefit of others—the disabled, in the case of punitive taxation of the unjust—would not be an injustice whenever the benefits are extracted from individuals who have, by voluntarily choosing to do that which they had no right to do, forfeited at least some portion of their right not to be used as means. Nozick's complaint against redistributive taxation, that it is a violation of self-ownership because it amounts to the forcing of people to come to the assistance of others, loses its sting when the tax is rendered so easily escapable and is imposed only on those who have chosen to do what they had no right to do.

III

Even someone who agrees with everything I have said up to this point might want to press the following objection to punitive taxation of the unjust.[13] It is likely that in order to raise the revenue necessary to pro-

---

[12] Hart, 'Prolegomenon', 21–2.

[13] I should note, however, that I am by no means convinced that taxation of the unjust must be regarded as punitive. Such taxation might instead be regarded as similar to the non-punitive taxation of luxury items or cigarettes and alcohol. It might be regarded as a schedule of fees that attach extra costs to certain choices that individuals might make. Unlike the case of alcohol, cigarettes, and luxury items, these would be choices they have no right to make. In order to highlight the difference between taxation of the unjust and punishment, we might leave our punitive

vide sufficiently generous assistance to the disabled one would have to impose very stiff fines on those who commit crimes. Such stiff taxation of criminals would be insensitive to the conviction, shared by many liberal egalitarians and libertarians, that there are strict upper limits to the amount of punishment that one can justifiably inflict in response to a given crime. It would be possible to raise enough revenue even while punishing those who have committed lesser crimes less severely than those who have committed more serious crimes. But, according to this objection, one could not raise enough money unless one punished criminals more severely than their crimes warrant.

This objection is sound only if there is good reason to endorse strict upper limits. Some would maintain that there are strict upper limits because there is a fixed and absolute amount of punitive harm that people deserve that is strictly proportional to the magnitude of their wrongdoing in each case. This rationale for strict upper limits should be rejected. Considerations having to do with social utility seem wholly appropriate as a factor in determining the magnitude of punishments, even when this results in punishments that seem out of proportion to the magnitude of the wrongdoing. Most do not object to the harsh punishment of hard-to-detect but relatively minor crimes, if such harsh punishment is the only economically feasible means of deterring that crime.[14] To take another example: there is nothing objectionable about increasing the penalty for a given crime that has become more of a social problem because its incidence has reached epidemic proportions, even though the fact that many others are committing the same crime that a given individual commits does not necessarily make the crime that that individual commits any more a wrong or harm.[15]

Perhaps a more promising rationale for strict upper limits appeals to the value of punishment as a means of communicating the appropriate level of society's condemnation of that crime.[16] Arguably,

---

practices intact and then assess the tax as an additional obligation of the convicted criminal whose magnitude does not correspond to the gravity of his crime but is rather assessed as a fixed lump sum or a fixed percentage of his wealth or income.

[14] Given the low probability that one will be detected, the *ex ante expected* disutility of punishment for committing a crime might be more in line with intuitions about proportionality than the *actual* disutility of punishment to those who are caught and convicted. I do not think, however, that *ex ante* expected disutility of being punished should be the measure of the magnitude of punishment for a given crime. Such a measure does not capture the genuine fact that those who are caught and convicted are treated much more harshly than those who are undetected and who end up having suffered nothing more than exposure to the risk of being punished.

[15] Cf. Warren Quinn, 'The Right to Threaten and the Right to Punish', *Philosophy and Public Affairs*, 14 (1985): 327–73, at 350.

[16] See Joel Feinberg, 'The Expressive Function of Punishment', *Monist*, 49 (1965): 397–423.

disproportionately high punishment would send the wrong message: namely, that the crime is worthy of greater condemnation than it is really worth. I grant that the punishment of more severe crimes more severely than less severe crimes might, in general, be necessary to communicate the relative moral seriousness of the various crimes. Nevertheless, there is no fixed absolute magnitude of punishment that expresses a given fixed absolute amount of condemnation. So long as the ordinal ranking of punitive taxes imposed on the unjust appropriately corresponds to the ordinal ranking of the seriousness of crimes, harsh punitive taxation of the unjust across the board need not send the wrong messages. If harsh across-the-board punishments were phased in slowly enough, we might not be shocked by, and might become accustomed to, these higher penalties in much the same way as we are not shocked by, and have become accustomed to, the fact that the prices of increasingly scarce items are much higher than they once were even after one adjusts for inflation. There are, no doubt, some limits on how severe or lax punishments can be without sending the wrong message. If all punishments were reduced to varying numbers of light slaps on the wrist—two for shoplifting, fifteen for grand theft, and forty for murder—they would express levels of condemnation that are too low across the board. By the same token, if all punishments, even for minor misdemeanours, were placed on a scale of increasingly painful and protracted methods of torture followed by execution, then the message would be too strong in all cases. Nevertheless, within lower and upper bounds, there is a fair amount of room for raising the magnitude of penalties across the board without sending the wrong message.

One might be able to produce other and better arguments for the claim that there are strict upper limits to the magnitude of justified punishment.[17] But, even if there are good grounds for this claim, liberal egalitarians and libertarians will not have any compelling objection to the assistance of the disabled through the taxation of the unjust within these limits. Even if the revenues raised within these limits are not sufficient to meet all of the claims of the disabled for assistance, and universal taxation must be imposed in order to make up the difference and meet these claims, any partial replacement of universal

---

[17] Warren Quinn, for example, argues that there are strict upper limits to the harm we may inflict in the form of punishment, and that these limits are the same as the intuitive upper limits to the harm an individual may inflict in self-protection to prevent someone from committing a crime against him. I am inclined to agree with Quinn on this point and to agree with the remarks he makes in justification of his intuitions regarding the extent of our rights of self-protection (see Quinn, 'The Right to Threaten and the Right to Punish', 346–50).

taxation with the taxation of the unjust would be a move in the direction of a more voluntary welfare state than the welfare state of traditional liberal-egalitarian theory—a welfare state, that is, that approaches that point at which it is sufficiently voluntary that even a libertarian could not object to its realization.

PART II

Punishment and Self-Defence

CHAPTER 3

The Right to Punish

In the previous chapter I enlisted the punitive practices of criminal justice to serve the redistributive ends of distributive justice. In this chapter I offer a Lockean justification of the natural right to punish. Such a justification is not only relevant to the case for making the unjust provide for the disabled that I presented in the previous chapter. Since the right of the government to punish is derived from the natural rights of individuals to punish, it is also relevant to the Lockean justification of political authority that I present in Part III of this book.

I

It is Locke's view that each person, upon reaching the age of majority, finds himself in 'a *state of perfect freedom*' (II. 4), which implies, among other things, rights to govern oneself.[1] These rights encompass, but also extend beyond, the familiar rights of autonomous persons in a liberal society to do as they please within the sphere of activities which concern only themselves. They include rights that are akin to those that governments possess. Among them is a right to punish violations of the 'law of nature', which proscribes the harming of 'another in his life, health, liberty, or possessions' (II. 6).[2] Moreover, each person comes into possession of a right to punish in accordance with his own interpretation of the specific content of the law of nature.[3] Hence, the

---

[1] In II. 118 Locke writes that '*a child is born a subject of no country or government*. He is under his father's tuition and authority, till he comes to age of discretion; and then he is a freeman, at liberty what government he will put himself under, what body political he will unite himself to'.

[2] On this right to punish see II. 7–8.

[3] In II. 87 Locke writes that 'Man being born . . . with a title to perfect freedom . . . hath by nature a power . . . to judge of, and punish the breaches of that law [of nature] in others, as he is persuaded the offence deserves'.

individual's right to punish is accompanied by a right to specify those acts that constitute crimes against the law of nature and to affix penalties to the commission of these acts.[4] Locke calls this latter right a right to legislate.[5]

Locke claims that the natural right to punish is justified as a necessary means of preventing violations of the law of nature:

> And that all men may be restrained from invading others rights, and from doing hurt to one another, and the law of nature be observed, which willeth the peace and *preservation of all mankind*, the *execution* of the law of nature is, in that state [of nature], put into every man's hands, whereby every one has a right to punish the transgressors of that law to such a degree, as may hinder its violation: for the *law of nature* would, as all other laws that concern men in this world, be in vain, if there were no body that in the state of nature had a *power to execute* that law, and thereby preserve the innocent and restrain offenders. (II. 7)[6]

It does not follow from the necessity of preventing rights violations that *everyone* must possess a right to punish. This rationale would equally justify the possession of this right by only a few, so long as they were able to preserve order. Locke believes that he can reach the conclusion that we *each* possess a right to punish in a state of nature by supplementing his argument from necessity with a claim of equality. Locke assumes that people are by nature one another's moral equals and argues that this equal status implies that each of us possesses this right to punish in a state of nature, since otherwise some would have rights to subordinate and impose their wills on others through punishment that others did not also possess in equal measure.[7] In short: since at least some must have the right to punish in

---

[4] The individual does not have *carte blanche* to specify whatever penalty he thinks fit. Such punishment must be 'proportionate to [the criminal's] transgression, which is so much as may serve for *reparation* and *restraint*' (II. 8).

[5] '[A] power to set down what punishment shall belong to the several transgressions which they think worthy of it' is, according to Locke, 'the *power of making laws*' (II. 88). Note that a right to punish need not be accompanied by a right to legislate. An individual could instead retain a right to punish, but only in accordance with a penal code that is imposed by a central government.

[6] The right to punish does not therefore automatically follow from a right of self-governance. One also needs to establish the necessity of punishment as a means of preventing rights violations. That is, I think, how it ought to be, since I believe that neither individuals nor the officials of legitimate governments would have the right to punish if punishment were either unnecessary or completely ineffective as a means of preventing rights violations. Here I am in agreement with Warren Quinn, who offers a neo-Lockean justification of a right to punish as implied by a natural right of individuals to self-protection (see Quinn, 'The Right to Threaten and the Right to Punish', *Philosophy and Public Affairs*, 14 (1985): 327–73).

[7] He writes in II. 7: 'And if anyone in the state of nature may punish another for any evil he has done, every one may do so: for in that *state of perfect equality*, where naturally there is no

order to preserve rights, then each must have the right to punish, or else the right to subordinate would not be held in equal measure, in violation of equality.[8]

II

The affirmation of a natural right to punish is controversial. Yet Locke maintains that such a right follows from a natural right of self-protection. This latter right is uncontroversial. Recently, Warren Quinn has offered a broadly neo-Lockean derivation of a natural right to punish from a natural right of self-protection. This derivation is noteworthy for its rigour and sophistication.[9] Quinn's justification of a right to punish is, I think, more convincing than the considerations which Locke himself offers in favour of this right. In this section I shall show that Quinn's justification of punishment is nevertheless vulnerable to a serious objection. I shall propose a revised version of his theory which overcomes this objection.

Quinn motivates the right to punish by means of considerations along the following lines:

1. You have a natural right to repel an aggressor by force if necessary—even by lethal force if that is necessary to prevent yourself from being killed or grievously injured.
2. You also have a natural right to protect yourself from grievous injury or death by building an unscalable wall around your dwelling.
3. Even if you could not build an unscalable wall, you would be entitled to build a wall that is too costly to scale. You would, for example, be entitled to place spikes that point outward on the top of the wall even if these spikes would not literally prevent the

superiority or jurisdiction of one over another, what any may do in prosecution of that law, every one must needs have a right to do.' Locke appears at times to argue that it follows from our natural equality that no one may be subordinated to or subjected to the will of any other in a state of nature (see II. 4, II. 54). But he could not have meant this, since this would be inconsistent with *anyone's* possessing a right to punish, as punishment involves subordination and subjection to the will of another. What he must have meant is that any rights to subordinate others must be held in equal measure by all.

[8] A similar Lockean argument could be deployed to establish that we each possess a right to legislate in a state of nature. The right to punish, which is necessary to preserve rights, is a right to do so in accordance with a schedule of penalties, and we must each possess a right to set the schedule of penalties (i.e. to legislate) if any possesses such a right, since otherwise we would not be one another's equals.

[9] Quinn, 'The Right to Threaten and the Right to Punish'.

would-be aggressor from scaling the wall but would deter him by making it too costly for him to do so. (Suppose that he could climb the wall only at the cost of painful wounds, and that aggressing against you wouldn't be worth such pain.)

4. But now let us suppose that you cannot, for some reason, install spikes that point outward, but only spikes that point inward, so that a would-be aggressor would injure himself on the way out rather than the way in. If this prospect of serious injury *after* he has aggressed against you would be sufficient to deter him, you have a right to install these inward-pointing spikes. This right follows from your right of self-protection. In other words, you have the right to make it the case that a would-be aggressor will be harmed if he harms you in order to deter him from harming you. And this is very close to a right to punishment.

According to Quinn's justification of punishment, a person's right to punish an aggressor who has violated (or has attempted to violate) his rights is derived from a right of this potential victim of such aggression to threaten the aggressor before the rights violation has occurred in order to try to deter him from violating his rights. This latter right to threaten is derived from the victim's right of self-protection *against that aggressor*.[10] Quinn, however, denies that a right of self-protection justifies the punishment of an aggressor solely on the ground that such punishment deters others from harming the victim of that aggression or others. He believes that punishment so justified would constitute a morally objectionable instance of using the punished individual as a means.[11]

Suppose that one derives a right to punish an aggressor only from a right of self-protection against that aggressor. It follows that a poten-

---

[10] Quinn writes: 'When we create threats of punishment we are, according to the theory I wish to develop, justified by our rights of *self-protection*. It is morally legitimate to create these threats because it is morally legitimate to try to protect ourselves in this way against violations of our moral rights . . . The theory asserts that a practice of punishment is at its moral core a practice of self-protective threats' (Quinn, 'The Right to Threaten and the Right to Punish', 336).

[11] Quinn, for example, strongly objects to the view that '[p]unished persons have no rights that stand against their punishment because, in part, punishing them is so often useful in helping to deter others from committing crimes' (ibid. 330). Quinn does not also object to the justification of the punishment of a person as a means of deterring *that person* (as opposed to others) from committing future crimes: 'It is clear, for instance, that in placing someone under a threat in hope of keeping him from crime, we are not using him . . . [T]hreatening a person so that he will act in certain ways and using him so that others shall act in certain ways involve quite different moral relations to his will. That a threat is designed to make the threatened party behave as he morally should is a fact that gives it, if not full justification, at least some moral support. However, the fact that an injury to someone helps keep others in line is almost nothing in its moral favor' (ibid. 345–6).

tial victim of aggression cannot justify punishment on ground of a right of self-protection against a particular aggressor if he knows that punishment that follows an irrevocable threat to punish if harmed makes no more contribution to his protection against that aggressor than a bluff (i.e. an insincere threat to punish if harmed). If we assume the soundness of Quinn's approach, then it appears that such punishment would violate the aggressor's right not to have normally rights-violating harm inflicted on him that the victim knows does not contribute to his (or anyone's) protection against that aggressor. If such punishment were justified, then it would have to be justified on a ground other than that of his right of self-protection against that aggressor, such as a right to use punishment as a means to deter others or a right of retribution.[12] I shall argue that such punishment *is* justified, and that it is justified on the former ground of general deterrence (when the pursuit of such deterrence is properly constrained by rights).[13]

I shall assume for the sake of argument throughout this section that aggressors never repeat their aggression.[14] If aggressors never repeat their aggression, then someone could not punish an aggressor to prevent that person from harming him (or anyone else) in the future. But he could punish that aggressor to prevent others from harming him or others in the future. Contrary to Quinn, I will show that (1) an individual can, on the very ground of a right to self-protection that Quinn ultimately relies upon to justify punishment, justify the punishment of an individual as a means of deterring others from committing crimes, and that (2) an individual or individuals (including government officials) can, on the ground of vindicating the right of protection that others possess, justify the punishment of an individual as a means of deterring others from committing crimes. Quinn's justification of the

---

[12] In addition to rejecting the former ground, Quinn rejects retributivism (see ibid. 331–5, 339). Quinn, however, rules out bluffing by the state on the ground that 'such deception would be morally insupportable. It is one thing for a private individual to protect himself by bluffing. But it is an altogether different thing for civic authorities, acting in their official capacities, to practice wholesale deception in a matter as vital as this to each citizen's interest' (ibid. 339). While I believe that deception is morally bad, I do not believe that it is so bad that it ought to be avoided at the cost of the infliction of punishment on an aggressor that does not enhance anyone's protection. Such punishment should strike a non-retributivist as gratuitous.

[13] I understand *general* deterrence to encompass the punishing of someone in order to provide people other than the punished person as well as the punished person with a reason to refrain from committing crimes in the future. *Specific* deterrence, on the other hand, would encompass only the punishing of someone in order to provide that person with a reason to refrain from committing crimes in the future.

[14] See ibid. 331, where Quinn entertains a similar assumption during the course of a discussion that is relevant to what I have to say below.

right to punish should therefore be revised to take these two claims on board.

In order to justify the two claims I have just made, I ask you to imagine someone who lives in a society in which his only means of protection against aggressors is a device that, when properly activated by his punching in the right code, automatically harms an aggressor if he harms him. It is impossible for him to demonstrate to others that he has punched in the right code. We might imagine that he must insert his arm into an iron sleeve in order to reach a hidden keyboard to punch in a code. Whenever he is confronted by an aggressor, he can pretend irrevocably to activate the device, or he can in fact irrevocably activate the device. Each time he is confronted by a new aggressor, he must activate the device anew. He is inalienably capable of bluffing in a manner that is indistinguishable from a genuine activation and therefore just as effective (or ineffective) a deterrent on any given occasion as such a genuine activation. If a genuine activation will be effective against a particular aggressor, then so will a bluff.

Imagine that this person is confronted by an aggressor who announces his intention to injure him.[15] Assume that the threatened party is committed to the moral proposition, which follows from Quinn's justification of punishment, that he is justified in punishing an aggressor on the ground that such punishment contributes to his self-protection against that aggressor but not on the ground that such punishment deters others. He correctly reasons that he is not justified, on the ground of self-protection against this particular aggressor, in activating the device. On this ground, he is justified only in bluffing, since activation provides him with no more protection against that aggressor than bluffing.[16] He will need to conceal this moral belief, since if an aggressor realizes that he thinks that he is morally committed to bluffing when confronted by an aggressor then his bluff will be called. Assume that he bluffs, the bluff fails even though he was able to conceal this moral belief, and he is injured.[17] Now this victim is confronted by a second aggressor, who has seen him bluff against the first aggressor. The second aggressor announces his intention to injure him. Having seen him bluff once, the aggressor suspects that the victim will bluff again, despite protests on his part to the contrary. Maintaining his commitment to his moral belief, the victim bluffs again, and the

---

[15] I shall assume throughout this section that aggressors are morally responsible for their behaviour.

[16] Let us also assume that he rejects Quinn's moral argument against deceptive threats (see n. 12 above).

[17] By hypothesis, activation would also have failed.

aggressor harms him.[18] He is then confronted by a third aggressor. He bluffs. Having witnessed his previous bluffs, the aggressor injures him. After he is confronted by a fourth, and fifth, a sixth, and a seventh aggressor, each of whom injures him following his bluff, he dies of multiple injuries. His commitment to his moral belief leads to his death because he cannot conceal, from someone who has witnessed his previous behaviour, his disposition to bluff that this belief creates.

Let us assume that he knows that if he had in fact activated the device when confronted by the first aggressor, the witnessing of the punishment of the first aggressor by subsequent aggressors would probably have been sufficient to deter all subsequent aggressors. He also knows that if, however, the second aggressor were not deterred by his punishment of the first aggressor, all subsequent aggressors would almost certainly have been deterred if they had witnessed his punishment of the first and second aggressors. I believe that he would have been straightforwardly justified on the ground of self-protection to use the first, and, if necessary, the second aggressors' punishment as a means of deterring subsequent aggressors, since he knew that such use of the first (or first and second) aggressor (or aggressors) would probably have made the difference between a single injury (or two injuries) to him and multiple injuries resulting in death.[19] I conclude that the right of self-protection, the very right to which Quinn appeals to construct a justification that rules out the using of the punishment of persons as a means to deter others, actually justifies the use of persons in this fashion.

Moreover, the victim in our story would also have been justified in using the punishment of individuals as a means of deterring other aggressors from injuring persons other than himself. In other words, he is morally permitted not only to use persons in order to protect himself against other persons, but also to use them in order to protect others against other persons. To see why this is so, let us imagine a different scenario in which the victim in our previous story is now fully shielded from injury. Others, however, are vulnerable to serial attacks by various aggressors.[20] Our former victim still controls the protective device, which can now be employed in order to try to deter aggressors from attacking these other vulnerable persons. Each of these potential

---

[18] Once again, by hypothesis, the aggressor also would have harmed him if he had, contrary to his moral beliefs, activated the device.

[19] That these aggressors are morally responsible for their behaviour is essential to this justification. I argue in the next chapter that one's right of self-protection does not justify the (lethal) harming of morally non-responsible aggressors.

[20] Recall that we are assuming that each aggressor aggresses only once.

victims endorses Quinn's justification of punishment (as I have interpreted it) and each chooses to delegate his privilege of vindicating his right of self-protection to the individual with the device, to whom I shall now refer as 'the protector'. If the aggressors reason and act as before, and the protector maintains the same sort of commitment to Quinn's justification, then the victims in our present story will be in a sorry predicament that resembles the predicament of our protector when he was a victim in the last story. For if the protector follows Quinn's justification and bluffs in the first instance, and, as before, the bluff fails to deter the first aggressor, then subsequent aggressors will repeatedly call the first and subsequent bluffs. The protector will be committed to bluff on each occasion, since on each occasion a bluff will contribute no less to the self-protection of a given individual against that aggressor than an activation of the device. Consequently, many, many aggressors later, each of the victims will lie dead of multiple injuries. I believe that, rather than follow Quinn's justification to this unhappy conclusion, the protector is morally entitled to activate the device in the first and subsequent occasions, not on Quinn's ground of vindicating anyone's right of self-protection against the particular aggressor who is threatened with punishment (since such vindication would not justify activation), but on the ground that it is permissible, in these instances, to use the punishment of aggressors as a means of deterring other aggressors from inflicting criminal harm on people, who have a right of protection against such harm.[21]

III

I shall conclude this discussion of Quinn's justification of punishment with some remarks on the implications of his theory regarding the punishment of the innocent. In particular, I shall consider the implications regarding the punishment of someone who is trying to kill another yet who is not morally responsible for his potentially lethal behaviour. I shall refer to such a person as an 'Innocent Aggressor'.[22] Suppose that someone whom you know to be an Innocent Aggressor will kill an innocent child unless you are able to prevent him from doing so. He will be prevented from killing this child if and only if he is deterred by the threat of death. Many would affirm the following conditional: if the activation of a device that would automatically kill

[21] For further defence of the above conclusions, see my 'Quinn on Punishment and Using Persons as Means', *Law and Philosophy*, 15 (1996): 201–8, at 206–8.
[22] I shall say more about the nature of Innocent Aggressors in the next chapter.

the Innocent Aggressor if he kills that child were the only thing which stands a decent chance of deterring him, then it would be justifiable to threaten to kill him by activating this device. If both this conditional and Quinn's theory were true, it would follow that it would be justifiable to execute such an Innocent Aggressor who has killed his intended victim in spite of the threat of the death penalty if such threat were the only thing which stood a decent chance of deterring him. But it is clearly unjust knowingly to execute an Innocent Aggressor, since it is unjust knowingly to execute the innocent. Hence, we must either reject Quinn's theory or reject the claim that it is justifiable, in the name of protecting the innocent child, to activate the aforementioned device. Many would affirm that a person may employ lethal means, including the activation of this device, against an Innocent Aggressor if this is necessary to prevent him from killing an innocent person. These people must reject Quinn's theory if they are to stand by their conviction that it is unjust knowingly to execute an innocent. In other words, we are confronted with a trilemma. We must reject at least one of the following three claims: (1) that it is just to use lethal means against an Innocent Aggressor if this is necessary to prevent him from killing an innocent person; (2) that it is unjust knowingly to execute an Innocent Aggressor; and (3) that Quinn's theory is sound. I am not prepared to repudiate (2), and I would like to vindicate the truth of (3). In order to do so, I need to reject (1). The following chapter constitutes a repudiation of (1).

CHAPTER 4

Killing the Innocent in Self-Defence

Many philosophers subscribe to the common belief that you are morally permitted to kill a person who endangers your life whenever such killing is necessary to prevent yourself from being killed. Such killing is thought to be permissible even when the endangering party is not morally responsible for endangering your life. In this chapter I argue that the intentional or foreseeable killing in self-defence of such an innocent person who is not about to die soon anyway is unjustifiable in circumstances in which it has been thought to be permissible.[1] More precisely, I argue that, with few exceptions, it is wrong to kill each of two types of dangerous person: an Innocent Aggressor and an Innocent Threat.[2]

An 'Innocent Aggressor' is a person who poses a danger to your life because she is acting from an intention to kill you. She remains innocent, however, since she is not responsible for her behaviour because, rather than proceeding from her character, it is explained by other factors completely beyond her control. An example of an Innocent Aggressor is someone who is pursuing you with a meat cleaver because she is moved by an uncharacteristic and overwhelming rage that has been induced by a powerful mind-altering drug that someone has slipped into her morning coffee.[3] By contrast, an 'Innocent Threat' is a person 'whose mere movements *qua* physical object or mere pres-

---

[1] Unless I indicate otherwise, the reader should assume that the innocent who endangers your life will die only if you defend yourself against her. Therefore, either you will die, or the person who endangers your life will die, and in no case will both you and she die if you do not defend yourself.

[2] Here I adopt, with some modifications, terms employed by Judith Jarvis Thomson in her 'Self-Defense', *Philosophy and Public Affairs*, 20 (1991): 283–310. Thomson defends the view (which I shall oppose) that it is permissible to kill both 'Innocent Threats' and 'Innocent Aggressors'. Her article provided the inspiration for this chapter.

[3] This scenario is modelled on a case that Thomson sketches (ibid. 284).

ence constitutes a threat to our life'.[4] Such a person is not responsible for her endangering presence or movements because they are not voluntary, intentional, or welcomed by her, and are the product of circumstances completely beyond her control. An example of an Innocent Threat is someone who has been pushed out of a tall building and will land on you and crush you to death (while surviving the fall herself) unless you vaporize her with your ray gun.[5]

Before presenting my case against the killing of Innocent Threats and Aggressors, I should note that I will not be advancing either of the following two claims. First, as I make clear in Section III below, my case against the killing of an innocent does not extend to one who is innocent of *blame* for trying to kill you but is nevertheless *morally responsible* for trying to kill you. Second, my case against the killing of an innocent does not extend to cases in which such killing is necessary to save a large number of lives rather than simply one's own life.

Much of my argument for the wrongness of killing a Threat or an Aggressor rests on the assumption that it is wrong to kill an Innocent Bystander in self-defence, where such a Bystander is someone who does not herself endanger your life and who is not responsible for whatever it is that does endanger your life.[6] In Sections I and II below I argue that killing a Bystander is, other things being equal, morally on a par with killing a Threat and that it is impermissible to kill a Bystander and hence impermissible to kill a Threat. In Section III I argue that the killing of an Aggressor is morally on a par with the killing of a Threat and hence also impermissible.

I

In this section and the next I shall defend the following argument for the impermissibility of killing a Threat:[7]

---

[4] Here I adopt Nancy Davis's formulation (see Davis, 'Abortion and Self-Defense', *Philosophy and Public Affairs*, 13 (1984): 175–207, at 190). She calls such threats 'passive threats'. Davis further explains that 'what renders someone a passive threat is not his or her immobility or inactivity, but his or her lack of agency: at least at the time of the attack, the person whose movements or presence poses a threat to someone's life is not an agent, but (in the old terminology) a patient' (ibid. 190 n. 36).

[5] This example is modelled on one of Robert Nozick's in his *Anarchy, State, and Utopia* (New York: Basic Books, 1974), 34.

[6] Unless otherwise noted, all references to Aggressors, Bystanders, and Threats are to those who are Innocent.

[7] For the purposes of this chapter, 'killing' will refer only to the initiation or sustaining of, or the insertion of somebody into, a sequence of events that results in the death of a person (cf. Philippa Foot, 'Killing and Letting Die', in Jay Garfield and Patricia Hennessey (eds.), *Abortion:*

P1 It is impermissible to kill a Bystander to prevent oneself from being killed. (I shall refer to this premiss as the *inviolability-of-a-Bystander thesis*.)

P2 The killing of a Threat and the killing of a Bystander are, other things being equal, on a par as far as permissibility is concerned.[8] (I shall refer to this premiss as the *moral-equivalence thesis*.)

Therefore, it is impermissible to kill a Threat to prevent oneself from being killed.

I turn first to a defence of the inviolability-of-a-Bystander thesis.

Most would agree that killing a Threat in self-defence cannot be justified on the ground that you may kill an innocent whenever such killing is necessary to save your own life, since it seems clear that you are not permitted to do so. If, for example, a javelin is headed toward you, and your only hope of survival is to grab an innocent stranger and use her body as a shield, such use of a Bystander is clearly not permitted.[9] In this case, you must harmfully *use* the Bystander's body in order to save yourself. Yet even in cases in which the Bystander's body is of no use to you, but you know that you will survive only if you initiate a sequence of events that you know will kill her, it is impermissible to do so. If, for example, the only way to prevent a projectile from killing you is to hurl a bomb at it that you know will also kill an innocent stranger, it is impermissible for you to hurl the bomb. To do

---

Moral and Legal Perspectives (Amherst, Mass.: University of Massachusetts Press, 1984), 179). It will not refer to instances of 'ducking harm' that result in the death of a person. It is, I think, permissible to duck out of the way of an oncoming javelin even if you foresee that, by ducking, you will allow the javelin to impale a Bystander standing behind you. It is, I think, also permissible to move out of the way of a falling Threat even if you foresee that so doing will result in that Threat's death (because she will hit hard concrete rather than soft flesh if you move away).

[8] Types of action are 'on a par as far as permissibility is concerned' just in case it is true that if any one of them is permissible then so are all the others, and if any one of them is impermissible then so are all the others.

[9] Moral constraints against the harming of Bystanders have the consequence that it is often impermissible to equalize the chances that innocents will suffer lethal harm. In the case just described, it is a matter of your bad luck, and the Bystander's good luck, that your location is such that you will live only if you impermissibly grab the Bystander, whereas her location is such that she will live if she permissibly does nothing. Some believe—in cases such as this one that include some number of people, none of whom bears any responsibility for the presence of a threat of lethal harm (whether the threat be a human being or a non-human object), and one of whom must be killed by this threat—that it is only fair that each bear an equal chance of being killed, if it is possible to equalize chances. By the logic of this argument from fairness, you would be entitled, after a favourable coin toss, to grab the unconsenting Bystander and use her body as a shield against the oncoming projectile. It is, however, impermissible to grab such a Bystander even after a favourable coin toss. If the moral-equivalence thesis is correct, it is also impermissible to vaporize a falling Threat even after a favourable coin toss.

so would, in Judith Jarvis Thomson's terminology, 'ride roughshod' over a Bystander.[10]

These judgements that it is impermissible to use or to ride roughshod over a Bystander strike me as, intuitively, highly plausible. Moreover, they are supported by the fact that they cohere with, or (given plausible auxiliary assumptions) are implied by, related moral judgements that appear to be at least as intuitively plausible. Most people think, for example, that you may not initiate a sequence of events that you foresee will kill one innocent, non-threatening person, even when so doing is necessary to save the lives of five others.[11] Philippa Foot, for example, has argued that you may not drive over one innocent recumbent person even if that is necessary for you to arrive in time to save five others from being swept away by a rising tide.[12] If you may not initiate such a sequence of events, how could you be permitted to initiate a sequence of events that you foresee will kill one Bystander when that is necessary to save merely one, even when that one is yourself? (Imagine that you must drive over one recumbent Bystander in order to prevent yourself from being swept away by a rising tide.) Are you permitted to give your own life such priority that you may take measures to save it that you could not take to save five strangers? I think not.

The condemnation of *using* a Bystander gains even greater support than the condemnation of running roughshod over a Bystander from the strength of the analogous claims that cohere with or imply the condemnation of using.[13] It would, for example, be particularly outrageous for you to push an innocent person on to the path of a trolley-car in order to prevent it from running over five others.[14] Special support through appeal to analogous cases can be found for

[10] See Thomson, 'Self-Defense', 289–92, 296, for a discussion to which I am indebted of cases involving the killing of Bystanders.

[11] Cases involving the redirection, as opposed to the initiation, of a lethal sequence of events (e.g. Philippa Foot's trolley-car problem) are a different matter. See section 6 of Thomson's 'The Trolley Problem', in her *Rights, Restitution, and Risk* (Cambridge, Mass.: Harvard University Press, 1986). See also Foot, 'Killing and Letting Die', 183.

[12] See Foot, 'Killing and Letting Die', 179–80. See also her 'Morality, Action, and Outcome', in Ted Honderich (ed.), *Morality and Objectivity* (London: Routledge and Kegan Paul, 1985), 24.

[13] I should note, however, that Thomson denies that it is, other things being equal, morally worse to use, rather than to ride roughshod over, a Bystander. She says: 'Appeals to the notion "respect for persons" will certainly not suffice to make out this special moral taint [of using a Bystander]. After all, if one proceeds in a . . . Riding-Roughshod-over-a-Bystander case, one behaves as if the person one kills were not there at all—surely no less a display of lack of respect for persons' ('Self-Defense', 291).

[14] The example is Thomson's (see her 'Killing, Letting Die, and the Trolley Problem', in *Rights, Restitution, and Risk*, 82–3).

condemning the use of a Bystander in cases in which one's use of the Bystander involves *initiating* a lethal sequence of events (as opposed to usefully inserting the Bystander into an already existing lethal sequence of events). Imagine that, instead of using a Bystander's body to shield yourself from an oncoming javelin, you must blow up the Bystander's body in order for the exploding body to knock the javelin off course. If this type of using of a Bystander is permissible, then it becomes difficult to resist the conclusion that it is also permissible to carve up a Bystander in order to transplant her organs into your ailing body, or that it is permissible to kill and eat a Bystander in order to save yourself from the threat of starvation. But such uses of the innocent are surely thought to be paradigm cases of the morally outrageous.

Given that the intentional or foreseen killing of an innocent in self-defence is unjustifiable when the innocent is a Bystander in the types of cases described above, how could it be justifiable when the innocent is a Threat in analogous circumstances? How, in other words, might one challenge the moral-equivalence thesis (a defence of which I now offer)? It is, of course, true that the Threat will kill you unless you kill her, whereas the Bystander will not. The most that a Bystander can be accused of is standing by and allowing you (rather than her) to be killed. Might one appeal to the doctrine that, other things being equal, killing somebody is harder to justify than merely allowing her to die, and infer from this doctrine that the Threat who will kill you unless you kill her is thus less worthy of immunity from being killed in your self-defence than the Bystander who does not endanger your life? I do not think so, since I believe that the moral distinction between killing and letting die gains plausibility from particular facts about the wrongness or moral evil of killings that are, or are the consequence of, intentional acts of morally responsible agents, especially when those acts are intended or foreseen as killings. It is natural to think that one bears special moral responsibility for such killings that flow from one's agency. No such special responsibility, however, plausibly attaches to lethal movements of one's body over which one has no control, as in the case of a Threat.

I believe that a related proposal advanced by Thomson to morally differentiate Threats and Bystanders can be rejected for similar reasons. Thomson says that 'what makes it permissible for you to kill [Threats] is the fact that they will otherwise violate your rights that they not kill you, and therefore lack rights that you not kill them'.[15]

---

[15] Thomson, 'Self-Defense', 302. Thomson's proposal is, in fact, motivated by her rejection of the suggestion that one may kill a Threat (but not a Bystander) because the Threat will kill you

On the other hand, it is clearly not the case that, unless they are killed, Bystanders will violate anybody's right not to be killed. I shall not dispute the inference Thomson draws from the premiss in the quoted passage. If, in fact, someone will violate your right not to be killed unless you kill her, this fact might be sufficient to justify your killing her. However, I do reject the premiss that if they kill you Threats will violate your right not to be killed.[16] Imagine cases involving Threats who endanger your life because they are falling from the sky as the result of forces completely outside human control. (Imagine that they have been lifted into the air by a tornado.) I agree with Thomson that it makes perfect sense to say that such a falling human being will kill you if she lands on you. I am willing to say that she will kill you even though she is without fault and lacks agency *qua* falling human being. Similarly, it makes perfect sense to say that a (faultless, agency-lacking) stone will kill you if it falls on you. But I find it difficult to make sense of Thomson's claim that such a falling human being will violate your right not to be killed if she falls on you. Surely one would not be tempted to make the same claim about a stone that falls on you after being lifted into the air by a tornado. Could things really be any different if it is an unconscious human being that falls on you after being lifted into the air by a tornado? I do not see how the rights-violating power of such a human object could be any greater than the

unless you kill her. She argues that if the fact that you will kill me unless I kill you were enough to justify my killing you, then I could kill you in self-defence even if I were a villain who was defensively fighting back against your attempt to kill me in justified self-defence against my initial villainous attempt to kill you. Thomson rightly rejects this consequence as absurd. She says that neither villains nor Threats may fight back against those who are defending themselves against being killed by them, and that they may not do so because those who would kill them in self-defence would violate no right of theirs by killing them. They would violate no right of the villain or the Threat because they kill in response to a *rights-violating* endangerment of their life by the villain or the Threat (see ibid. 303–5).

[16] Before disputing this premiss, I would like to note a different problem with Thomson's rights–based approach to self-defence. In the case of a Threat who is falling toward you, Thomson maintains that if you kill her you do not violate her right not to be killed because she has, by virtue of the fact that she is threatening your right not to be killed, already lost her right not to be killed. There is, on Thomson's account, a moral asymmetry between you and the falling Threat that is explained by the fact that she endangers your life first. Thomson's account runs into difficulties when we eliminate the asymmetry. Consider a case (which I owe to Gary Gleb) in which I am innocently falling toward a net and so are you. We are also each falling toward each other and will fatally collide before we reach the net unless one or the other of us is eliminated. Conveniently, each of us has a ray gun whose beam can vaporize the other, thus clearing the shooter's path to the net. May I shoot my ray gun on Thomson's account? Only if I possess a right not to be killed that you will violate unless I kill you. Do I possess such a right? Only if I do not threaten to violate a right of yours not to be killed. Do you possess such a right? Only if you do not threaten to violate a right of mine not to be killed, etc. It is difficult to determine, on Thomson's account, whether either possesses a right that the other will violate, and hence whether either may shoot in self-defence.

rights-violating power of a chunk of granite. But talk of rights violations has, I think, gone too far if it is based on a theory that implies that
a falling stone can violate a human right.

Frances Kamm has argued that there *is* a moral difference between a
faultless, unconscious, falling human person and a falling stone. She
believes that the former, but not the latter, violates the right of the
individual on whom she falls.[17] She argues:

> The position of [a Threat] is different from that of a natural object—for exam-
> ple, a stone that the wind hurls at a person—because she is not a stone but,
> rather, a person who should not be in an inappropriate position relative to
> others. One person's inappropriate location vis-à-vis another raises moral
> questions no matter how it comes about, whereas the unfortunate location of
> an object does not . . . One simply has a right not to have someone on the
> body or property to which one is entitled, even if the wind put them there.[18]

Why is it that a person, but not a stone, should not be in an inappropriate location? I believe that in so far as we possess Kamm's intuition
that a person can violate your right by falling on you, it is because we
think that a person is capable of taking precautions to avoid being in
that inappropriate location and is capable of knowing that she should
take such precautions. But this rationale will not do, since Kamm and
others believe that you may destroy a falling Threat even when she
falls after having been kidnapped and rendered unconscious by a villain. Kamm presumably also believes that you may destroy a falling
human being who normally possesses as strong a right not to be killed
as any other human being even if that falling human being is an infant.
Yet I cannot imagine how one could successfully argue that it is possible for an infant, but impossible for a stone, to violate your right by
landing on you.

Nothing that I have said thus far should be construed as denying
that there are cases in which it is *because* of a stone falling on you that
your right has been violated. We can easily imagine cases in which
somebody is morally responsible for dropping a stone on you. In
those cases, your right not to be killed has been violated. But it does
not follow that the *stone*, rather than the morally responsible person,
has violated your right. Consideration of an analogous case might
shed light on this point. If you are killed by an assassin's bullet, you

[17] See Kamm's defence of the killing of Threats in Kamm, *Creation and Abortion* (New York:
Oxford University Press, 1992), 45–50. Perhaps Kamm does not go so far as to claim that the
falling Threat *violates* a right of the person on whom she falls. At the very least, however, she
claims that the falling Threat *causes* a right of the person on whom she falls to be violated. I
believe that my response counters either claim. See my rejection below of this distinct claim.

[18] Ibid. 47.

are also killed by the assassin, but it is only the assassin, and not the bullet, that has violated your right not to be killed, even though it is because of the bullet's killing you that the assassin has violated your right not to be killed.

In the light of this, Thomson's claim might be modified in the following manner.[19] Rather than claim, as Thomson does, that the falling Threat violates your right, one might advance the weaker claim that the falling Threat *causes* a right of yours to be violated. This latter claim might seem more plausible than the former in the case of lethal objects that lack agency. One might make the further claim that you are permitted to kill a Threat just in case, and because, it will otherwise cause a violation of your right not to be killed.

The arguments against the claim that human beings transformed into Threats by forces totally outside human control can *violate* rights can also be employed to counter the claim that such human beings can *cause* rights violations. I am no more convinced by the claim that a naturally falling stone such as a meteorite can cause a rights violation than I am by the claim that such an object can violate a right.[20] Since, as I have argued above, human Threats falling as the result of forces completely outside human control are morally indistinguishable (except in so far as it would be worse to destroy them) from falling non-human objects (such as meteorites) whose trajectory is completely outside human control, I resist the claim that such falling Threats can cause a rights violation.

It might nevertheless be possible in other cases for a falling Threat to cause a rights violation. A Threat could, for example, be a means by which a morally responsible agent violates a right (much as the assassin's bullet is a means by which the assassin violates her victim's right not to be killed). Imagine such a case in which a falling Threat will, by landing on you, cause the violation of your right not to be killed, and that she will cause such a rights violation because a villain has pushed her out of a tall building in order to kill you. Might this Threat lose her right not to be killed because, and just in case, she will otherwise cause your right not to be killed to be violated? I do not think so. If a gust of wind had hurled this Threat in your direction, the Threat could not have caused any rights violation whatsoever and hence could not have lost her right not to be killed. It would be very odd, however, to conclude that the human being whose rights were violated by her being

---

[19]   The following modification was suggested by Seana Shiffrin.

[20]   Here I am not, of course, talking about cases in which a meteorite is an indirect cause of a rights violation because, say, someone insured against such a catastrophe and the insurer culpably refuses to make good this claim.

thrown out of the window, by then innocently causing a rights violation consequently loses her right not to be killed, whereas the human
being blown by the wind retains her right not to be killed. Why should
the fact that a villain, rather than the wind, has sent someone flying
strip that person of her moral immunity from being killed? If anyone
should lose her immunity from being killed, surely it is the villainous
rights-violator rather than the innocent causal mechanism through
which the villain violates the right.

Another way of differentiating the moral status of Threats and
Bystanders appeals to the notion of persons as enjoying sovereignty
over their own 'space'.[21] Perhaps the fact that a Threat will invade
your space whereas a Bystander will not is sufficient to justify the
claim that you may kill a Threat whereas you may not kill a Bystander.
If, however, what I have said above is correct, then you cannot complain that the Threat will violate (or cause the violation of) your right
over your own space, since such a suggestion would be vulnerable to
the same sort of objection that applied to the proposal that the Threat
may be killed because she would otherwise violate (or cause the violation of) your right not to be killed. If, on the other hand, you cannot
object that the Threat will violate your right over your own space,
then it is not clear that you possess the sort of moral objection to the
Threat's movement that would justify your intentionally killing her.[22]
Indeed, whether or not invading your space constitutes a rights violation, the fact that someone will invade your space is not by itself
sufficient to justify a violent response, much less lethal force. Imagine,
for example, that a small child has somehow been handcuffed and
strapped to your body and will remain attached for the next few min-
utes. Whether or not such an invasion of your space constitutes a
rights violation, surely you may not vaporize the child even if that is
the only way to stop her from occupying your space. At best, you
could respond in such fashion only if your being attached to the child
were killing you or causing serious injury. But now the fact that the
child will kill (or injure) you grounds the claim that you may kill her,
and not the fact that she will invade your space. I have, however,
already argued that such a person could not be said to violate your
right not to be killed if she kills you in this fashion. The mere fact that

[21] This line of argument was suggested by an anonymous reader. For the relevance of the idea
of sovereignty over one's space to the case for killing a Threat in self-defence see sections I and
II of Thomson, 'A Defense of Abortion', in *Rights, Restitution, and Risk*.

[22] For one thing, Thomson's 'fighting-back' objection (see n. 15 above) would apply. If one is
justified in killing simply because one's space will be invaded, then a villain would be justified in
fighting back against my attempt to defend myself against that villain's initial attack, since my
attempt to defend myself would invade the villain's space.

a Threat, but not a Bystander, will kill you unless you kill her is also not enough to differentiate a Threat from a Bystander and justify the killing of the former but not the latter.

One might, finally, argue that, even if a Threat cannot be said to violate either your right not to be killed or your right over your space, and even if the mere fact that the Threat will kill you is insufficient to justify your killing her, nevertheless, the *combination* of the fact that the Threat will kill you *and* that she will invade your space is sufficient to justify your killing her. I do not believe, however, that the fact that in addition to killing you a Threat will also invade your space is of such moral significance. Imagine that you and an unconscious stranger have been kidnapped and placed inside an airtight chamber. You know that the chamber will be opened in the near future. You also know that there is enough air for the two of you to survive in the meantime if and only if each of you breathes normally. If, however, the stranger takes an enormous breath, the stranger will live and you will die of oxygen deprivation. You notice that the unconscious stranger is about to take an enormous breath. May you shoot her? Intuitively, it strikes me that the case for shooting in these circumstances is no less strong than the case for shooting in those circumstances in which the Threat will kill you by falling on you (rather than by breathing the oxygen that surrounds you). I therefore doubt that the fact that a Threat will invade your space contributes much, if at all, to a justification of your killing that Threat in self-defence.

To summarize: An appeal to the mere fact that Threats but not Bystanders will kill you unless you kill them is not sufficient to justify the claim that Threats but not Bystanders may be killed in self-defence. I reject the claim that Threats can be distinguished from Bystanders because they but not Bystanders will violate, or cause the violation of, your right not to be killed by killing you. Finally, an appeal to the fact that Threats but not Bystanders will invade or continue to occupy your space unless you kill them is not sufficient to justify the claim that Threats may be killed in self-defence.

I shall now present a positive defence of the moral-equivalence thesis. I propose that Threats and Bystanders *share* an important morally relevant property that presents a prima-facie case for the impermissibility of killing in both cases. This property is that of being a 'bystander' *qua* responsible agent to the object that poses a danger to life. I believe that the moral property that explains why we may not kill a Bystander is her lack of responsible lethal agency, and not the absence of her body from the sequence of events that results in death. I have defined a Bystander as somebody who does not herself endanger your life and who is not responsible for whatever it is that endangers your life. By this definition a Threat is not, strictly speaking, a Bystander, since a Threat endangers your life: she will kill you unless you kill her. We must, however, distinguish ways in which one can kill somebody. One can kill another as the result of the exercise of one's morally responsible agency or merely by means of movements of one's body that do not proceed from one's agency. The Threat kills only in the latter sense: *qua* human body rather than *qua* agent. Even though a Threat is not, strictly speaking, a Bystander in the technical sense that I have introduced, nor is she literally a bystander to her body, she is a bystander in the morally relevant sense because she is a bystander *qua* agent (and hence *qua* responsible agent) to the endangering movements or presence of that body. Like a Bystander, the Threat is a bystander *qua* agent because that which endangers another's life is neither an action of hers nor the consequence of any action of hers. As an illustration of the claim that a Threat is a bystander *qua* agent, imagine that a villain has drugged an individual, temporarily paralysing her. The villain then proceeds to use her body as a club against an innocent victim. The innocent person trapped inside this body that has been transformed into a weapon would be reduced to a mere onlooker to the lethal motion of her body, someone who is not in control of, and is in fact alienated from, her body *qua* endangering object.

Support for my positive defence of the moral-equivalence thesis can be found in a comparison of the following cases: First imagine that an innocent person is lying alongside the path of a runaway trolley-car. Unless you hurl at that trolley-car a bomb that you know will also kill the innocent person, the trolley-car will run you over. Given what I have said about the impermissibility of killing a Bystander, it would not be permissible for you to destroy the trolley-car. Now imagine a second case in which the same person is trapped inside a runaway trolley-car. Unless you hurl a bomb that will destroy the trolley-car, and hence also the innocent person, the trolley-car will run you over before coming to a gentle stop. If doing that which foreseeably will kill the person is impermissible in the case in which the person is alongside the trolley-car, then I do not see how it could be permissible if the person is inside the trolley-car. Merely changing the location of the person should not make any moral difference in this case. If, however, it is impermissible to destroy the trolley-car inside which a person is trapped, then I do not see how it could be permissible in a third case to vaporize a falling body that itself constitutes a Threat. The only factual difference between the second case and the third that might lend support to the claim that it is permissible to kill in the third case but not the second is that in the third case it is the person's body that will kill you, whereas in the second case it is rather the trolley-car in which the person is encased that will kill you. But this sort of difference lends no support to the claim that it is permissible to kill in the third case but not the second, for two reasons. First, as I have argued previously, no sound moral rationale has yet been advanced for the principle that the unavoidable insertion of one's body into a lethal sequence of events strips one of one's moral immunity from being killed. Second, the general application of this principle is not supported by intuitions about cases. Rather, the application of this principle generates intuitively bizarre results. By this principle, even if it would, for example, be impermissible to kill a falling person if it were only the mass of the enormous ski boots attached to her feet that would kill you, it would be permissible to kill her if it were, instead, the mass of her body that would kill you. There seems, however, to be no morally relevant difference between these cases.

Those, such as Thomson, who believe that it is permissible for you to kill the falling Threat but impermissible for you to do that which you know will kill the Bystander lying alongside the trolley-car are faced with the following dilemma. If they believe that it is permissible for you to destroy the trolley-car inside which an innocent person is trapped, then they must perform the difficult task of explaining why an innocent inside a trolley-car may be killed, whereas one who is near the trolley-car may not. However, if they believe that it is impermissible for you to destroy the trolley-car with the trapped innocent, then they must explain why such an innocent may not be killed whereas a Threat that is falling toward you may be. My own view is that killing a person alongside the trolley-car, killing a person inside the trolley-car, and killing a falling Threat are on a par as far as permissibility is concerned. The very property—of being not responsible for that which threatens the life of another—that makes it impermissible to kill the innocent person alongside the trolley-car is also present in the cases of the innocent person inside the trolley-car and the falling Threat, thus providing us with a prima-facie reason to conclude that killing is impermissible in these other two cases as well. Moreover, I have argued that there are no other morally relevant properties pulling in the other direction in each of these latter two cases (but absent in the former case) that provide us with any reason to override this prima-facie reason.[23]

[23] I have not claimed that (*a*) the factual difference in the location and in the causal efficacy of the body are each of such *slight* moral significance as to not make the difference between

Not only is it impermissible to kill the Threat as well as the Bystanders in the cases just described, but, if anything, the vaporization of the falling Threat is morally *worse* than the destruction of a person inside, or alongside, the trolley-car. In the latter two cases the destruction of a human being is of no use to you. You use the destruction of the trolley-car as the means to save your life, and the destruction of a human being is merely the foreseen consequence of this useful destruction. But when you vaporize the body of the falling Threat, your killing of an innocent person is a *means* to save your life rather than merely a *foreseen consequence*. Here your vaporization is analogous to the worst type of killing of a Bystander, in which you initiate a lethal sequence of events that will result in the useful destruction of a Bystander.[24] It is also analogous to those most deplorable cases in which you kill a Bystander in order to eat her body to prevent yourself from starving or in order to replace your failing vital organs with her healthy ones. The vaporization of the Threat is a means to your end of saving your life even though the falling Threat is, as I have argued, a bystander *qua* agent to her lethally falling body.[25] It does not follow from the fact that an innocent person is alienated *qua* agent from her body that she is literally a bystander to her body such that one may intend to destroy her body without intending to destroy her, as one could if, say, her body were a heavy life-support system to which she was attached by a long ethereal cord. Whether the relation is one of constitution, identity, or something else, the relation between her body and her is sufficiently intimate that one could not intend to destroy her body as a means to save one's own life without intending to destroy her as well.[26]

impermissibility and permissibility by itself. Nor have I fallaciously inferred that a combination of slight moral differences cannot amount to a difference between impermissibility and permissibility. Rather, I have claimed that (*b*) neither factual difference is of any assistance in making a case for the permissibility of killing a Threat. In addition, I plausibly assume that (*c*) there is no good reason to believe that the combination of the two factual differences—each of which, by itself, makes no positive contribution to the case for permissibility—might somehow synergistically give rise to a case for permissibility. From claims (*b*) and (*c*) I can infer that there is no morally relevant difference between the first and third case that would ground the claim that it is permissible to kill in the third case even though impermissible in the first.

[24]   Recall my previous categorization of 'use-of-a-Bystander' cases into those that involve the useful insertion of a Bystander into an already existing lethal sequence of events and those that involve the initiation of a new sequence of events that usefully destroys the Bystander.

[25]   I am indebted to Timothy Hall for making and defending this point.

[26]   In her 'The Problem of Abortion and the Doctrine of Double Effect' Foot says that it would be absurd to maintain that one could aim to blow a person into small bits without also aiming to kill that person (see Foot, *Virtues and Vices* (Berkeley, Calif.: University of California Press, 1978), 21–2). Moreover, Timothy Hall has suggested to me that even if it were somehow possible to intend to destroy *X*'s body without intending to destroy *X*, the relation between *X* and *X*'s body might nevertheless be so intimate that intending to destroy *X*'s body would be morally on a par with intending to destroy *X*.

II

I would now like to consider two objections to the argument I have presented in Section I above.

1. In addition to presenting a defence of the moral-equivalence thesis, I have employed the intuition that it is impermissible to kill a Bystander as a fulcrum by means of which to dislodge the intuition that it is permissible to kill a Threat. Reversing this line of argument, one who endorses the moral-equivalence thesis might try to employ the intuition that it is permissible to kill a Threat as a fulcrum by means of which to dislodge the intuition regarding the impermissibility of killing a Bystander.

I would resist this reversal for two reasons. First, I believe that the intuitive judgement that it is impermissible to kill a Bystander is both more strongly held, and more central to our deontological morality, than the intuitive judgement that it is permissible to kill a Threat. A second, related point is that the judgement that it is impermissible to kill a Bystander gains support by virtue of the fact that it coheres with or is implied by a host of related, and at least as firmly held, intuitive judgements (spelled out in Sect. I above) about the wrongness of killing innocents. These judgements about the wrongness of harming some to save others, and about the wrongness of using people, are at the core of our deontology. The revision of our judgement that it is impermissible to kill a Bystander would therefore be quite costly. On the other hand, the judgement that it is permissible to kill a Threat is not similarly central to our deontology. Rather, it makes a puzzling exception to the deontological prohibition against the killing of the innocent. Moreover, it does not gain as much support from strongly held, and deontologically central, judgements. The judgement, for example, that it is permissible to kill a villainous aggressor in self-defence might be as strongly held and nearly as central to our deontological morality as the judgements about the impermissibility of killing innocents with which our judgement about killing Bystanders coheres. But this judgement about killing villainous aggressors neither implies nor coheres with the judgement that it is permissible to kill a Threat, since such aggressors are easily distinguishable from Threats by the morally relevant property of being villainous rather than innocent. There are, however, certain strongly held judgements about the permissibility of killing certain types of aggressor such as soldiers and other morally responsible agents who are innocent of blame for what they do, and these judgements might plausibly be thought to cohere with or imply the judgement that it is permissible to kill a Threat. I argue in Section III below that these judgements also do not imply or cohere with the judgement that it is permissible to kill a Threat. Hence, revising the judgement that it is permissible to kill a Threat is significantly less costly than revising the judgement that it is impermissible to kill a Bystander.[27]

2. The following might be presented as a counter example to the conclusion of my argument. Imagine that you are holding a flagpole upright out of patriotism for your country.[28] You come to realize that if and only if you do nothing but continue to hold this flagpole, a falling Threat will be impaled on the pole, but you will be unharmed. If you drop the flagpole, then the Threat will land on you, killing you but surviving the fall herself. May you continue to hold the flagpole? Many would insist that you may. But, by so doing, do you not kill the Threat by sustaining a lethal sequence of events? Is it not the case that if you may not shoot and vaporize a falling Threat in order to save your life, then you may not continue to hold the flagpole in order to save your life?

I am prepared to swallow, as a consequence of my argument, the claim that you may not continue to hold the flagpole. I do not believe that continuing to hold the flagpole is, except perhaps trivially, morally less bad than shooting one's ray gun. You are, in this case, sustaining rather than initiating a lethal sequence of events. But your primary intention in shooting the ray gun and in continuing to hold the flagpole is the same: to prevent, by lethal means, the Threat from falling on you. The fact, in the flagpole case, that you continue to do something that you were previously doing only for benign reasons is insufficient to remove the moral taint. Consider, for example, a related case in which you are benignly driving your car down a country road. You spot a hated in-law lying unconscious on the road ahead of you. If you continue to drive down the road, but now for the purpose of running over your in-law, the fact that you continue to do something that you were

---

[27] Even if what I have said in defence of the inviolability-of-a-Bystander thesis is unconvincing, and I have succeeded only in defending the moral-equivalence thesis, I still have demonstrated something of moral significance. For if the moral-equivalence thesis is true, then, whether or not the inviolability-of-a-Bystander thesis is true, one must accept the disturbing consequence that either of two fairly well-entrenched intuitions is false: we must reject either our intuition that it is permissible to kill a Threat or our intuition that it is impermissible to kill a Bystander.

[28] This is a slightly modified version of an objection suggested by Seana Shiffrin.

previously doing only for benign reasons does nothing to remove the moral taint of your action. Running over your in-law would be no less bad, except perhaps trivially, than it would be in a case in which you see your in-law lying unconscious on the street near your home and start the engine of your car in order to run her over. The fact, in the case of your continuing to hold the flagpole, that this action might be overdetermined by some benign reason in addition to your intention to impale the Threat is also, I think, morally irrelevant. Imagine that you continue to hold the flagpole in order both to impale the Threat and to prevent the American flag from touching the ground. Surely, this form of overdetermination is not enough to erase the moral taint—no more so than in a case in which you continue to drive down the country road in order both to run over your in-law and to return a videotape that you have rented.

III

I have said enough by now to cast serious doubt on the claim that it is permissible to kill a Threat. I now turn to the more difficult task of casting doubt on the claim that it is permissible to kill an Aggressor. Some maintain that killing in self-defence, while permissible against an Aggressor, is impermissible against a Threat. It is, however, difficult to justify such an asymmetry in the moral status of the Aggressor versus the Threat. The only potentially morally relevant fact that distinguishes Aggressors from Threats is the presence of harmful agency: the Aggressor acts from an intention to harm her victim, whereas the Threat does not. I believe, however, that the presence or absence of harmful agency is morally relevant only in cases involving those who are functioning as morally responsible agents. Yet Aggressors and Threats are, by hypothesis, not functioning as morally responsible agents. I believe, therefore, that the presence or absence of harmful agency is morally irrelevant in these cases.

I have defined an Aggressor as a person who acts from an intention to kill you but who is innocent of responsibility for her behaviour because rather than proceeding from her character, it is explained by other factors completely beyond her control. If we define a lethal agent as somebody who acts from an intention to kill you, then the category of Aggressor does not include all lethal agents who are innocent of blame for what they do, since it does not, for example, include persons who act from an intention to kill you, who are morally responsible for doing so, but who are nevertheless innocent of blame for what they do. The category of Aggressor does not, for example, include an innocent lethal agent who is acting from an intention to kill you in self-defence, where such action is a rational and avoidable response to her justified (but false) belief that you are a villain who is about to kill her. (Imagine that you extend your hand to shake the hand of some foreign dignitary at a reception. Unbeknown to you, a third party projects a stunningly realistic holographic image of a pistol on to your hand. The dignitary, who is accustomed to threats on her life, sees the hologram, forms the justified belief that you are about to assassinate her, and coolly draws a pistol in order to shoot you down in self-defence.) I believe that, in this type of case, you may kill in self-defence because you are killing in response to the action of an agent who is morally responsible in the following respects: the action that endangers your life flows from an agent who identifies with the intention from which she acts, is of sound mind when she acts, and could have avoided endangering your life. Unlike Threats and Aggressors, a morally responsible agent may be held accountable for engaging in such activity that puts the life of a potentially innocent person at risk even if she acts from the justifiable (but false) belief that this person is a villain. When one is in possession of rational control over such a dangerous activity as the shooting of a gun at somebody, it is not unfair that, if the person one endangers happens to be inno-cent, one is by virtue of engaging in such dangerous activity stripped of moral immunity from being killed. A responsible agent takes a gamble by placing this moral immunity on the line when she engages in such avoidable risky activity. It is, on the other hand, unfair to strip an Aggressor or a Threat of moral immunity from being killed if she endangers the life of another, since she exerts no rational control over her endangering activity.[29]

Contrary to what I have just said, one might insist that the exercise of morally non-responsible as well as morally responsible lethal

[29] Does my opposition to the killing of Innocent Aggressors imply pacifism? Probably not. Even if they are innocent of blame for what they do, many soldiers are not Innocent Aggressors, since they are morally responsible for what they do. Even if some soldiers are, properly speak-ing, Innocent Aggressors, cases of warfare must still be distinguished from the cases that I have discussed in this chapter, all of which were cases in which numbers did not tip the balance, since all were cases of one life versus one life, with no further consequences. Numbers may justify the killing of soldiers in wartime even if they are Innocent Aggressors. Like most deontological con-straints, the constraint against killing the innocent in self-defence is not absolute. Warfare creates an atmosphere of emergency and catastrophe in which ordinary deontological constraints begin to lose their grip. If we allowed ourselves to be defenceless in the face of a malevolent enemy leadership that operates through the agency of Aggressors or protects itself and manipulates its opponent through the use of innocent shields and hostages, then the constraint against the killing of Aggressors would be observed at too high a price.

agency is sufficient to strip a person of her moral immunity from being killed. One might believe that the mere presence of lethal agency is sufficient to ground the claim that the endangering party will violate the right of her victim not to be killed. One might accept the claim advanced in Section I above that a Threat cannot violate your right not to be killed yet resist the further claim that an Aggressor also cannot violate your right not to be killed.[30] Even one who is convinced that an unconscious, falling human object cannot violate your right might wonder whether the same can be said of a morally non-responsible psychotic who wishes you dead, plots your murder, stalks you, and finally kills you in cold blood. I do not think, however, that the presence of lethal agency is, in the absence of morally responsible agency, sufficient to ground an instance of a rights violation. An angry grizzly bear on the attack against a human being possesses some of the marks of an Aggressor: it lacks moral responsibility for what it does, yet it acts in order to harm. Yet there is little temptation to claim that a grizzly bear can violate your right not to be killed.

It is significant that even though few are convinced that grizzly bears can violate the rights of human beings, most of us are convinced that a human being may, in self-defence, kill a grizzly bear on the attack. I believe that the correct explanation of why it is justifiable for a human being to kill an attacking grizzly bear also provides an explanation of why it is in fact morally permissible for a human being to kill certain types of lethal human agents in self-defence, even if such agents are incapable of violating any rights and hence cannot be killed on the ground that they will otherwise violate rights. The simple explanation of why you may kill a lethal agent that happens to be a grizzly bear on the attack is that you are a human person, whereas it is merely a grizzly bear, and human persons are worth more than grizzly bears. I believe that the same can be said about a contest between a normal human person and certain types of psychotic. A normal human being is worth more than a human being whom mental illness has permanently rendered incapable of moral agency.

I announced at the beginning of this chapter that I would argue that the killing in self-defence of an Aggressor is unjustifiable. Such a claim is consistent with the claim I have just advanced—that it is permissible to kill certain types of lethal human agents in self-defence—since I do not believe that dangerous psychotics who have been permanently ravaged by certain types of mental illness are persons. Yet an

---

[30] This point and the following points also apply to claims about the mere causation of a rights violation as well as to claims about the violation of a right.

Aggressor is, by definition, a person. In my selection, at the beginning of this chapter, of an example to illustrate the concept of an Aggressor I was careful to describe a case involving a human being who did not permanently fall below the threshold of personhood. Recall that this individual was *temporarily* rendered a psychotic Aggressor by a drug that had been slipped into her morning coffee. I do not believe that one is justified in killing such an Aggressor in self-defence, since the innocent human person persists in the body of a temporarily psychotic Aggressor, just as an innocent human person normally persists in a body that has momentarily been transformed into a dangerous projectile by a gust of wind or that has been rendered temporarily unconscious. A person does not, however, persist in the body of one who has been permanently and irreversibly ravaged by certain types of severe mental illness, who has fallen into a permanent vegetative state, or who has died. There is, in these cases, no interest of a person that could be weighed against the life of a person whom that human being or body might endanger.

We can see now that my claim that it is impermissible to kill a Threat or an Aggressor does not generalize to the claim that one must refrain from killing morally responsible but innocent lethal agents, or that one must be a pacifist, or that one must refrain from killing incorrigibly psychotic killers. As I noted in Section II above, the cost of giving up our intuition that it is permissible to kill Threats (and, I should now add, Aggressors) is not as great as the cost of giving up our intuition that it is impermissible to kill Bystanders.

I believe that it will be easier to revise the intuition that it is permissible to kill a Threat or an Aggressor once one fully internalizes the fact that the moral status of the innocent human person trapped in the falling Threat or the temporarily psychotic Aggressor is on a par with the moral status of other types of innocent persons to whom one happily grants deontological immunity from being killed. The mere fact that the one first endangered the life of the other is not sufficient to grant the other the moral licence to kill the person that is trapped in the body of the Threat or the Aggressor. It is, of course, horrible when a Threat or an Aggressor kills an innocent human person, just as it is horrible when an innocent human person is killed by a natural event. But such a killing by an Aggressor or a Threat is, by hypothesis, not one for which the Threat or the Aggressor is morally responsible, nor is it an injustice. If the innocent victim of such a Threat or Aggressor cannot help but instinctively and lethally strike back in the heat of the moment, then she may be excused on the grounds that she is not a morally responsible agent at that moment either. But if, unlike the

Threat or the Aggressor, she is able *qua* responsible agent to collect herself and deliberately execute the annihilation of this other person, she will have no excuse for this unjustifiable exercise of her moral agency. All moral bets are not off when one's life is endangered. Just as it is inexcusable to sacrifice the life of a Bystander to defend oneself in the heat of the moment, it is inexcusable to sacrifice the life of a Threat or an Aggressor to defend oneself.

PART III

Political Society

CHAPTER 5

Political Society as a Voluntary Association

Under what conditions, if any, does a government have legitimate political authority over those whom it governs? In this chapter and the next I offer a left-libertarian reconstruction and defence of John Locke's answer to this question. To set the stage in a Lockean fashion, I take *government* roughly to be the set of institutions that collectively retains a monopoly on the powers of legislation and punishment over those who occupy the territory over which it claims dominion.[1] I take *political society* roughly to be a group of individuals in a given territory who are subject to the control of a single government. I take the *legitimate political authority* of a government chiefly to include the following rights to legislate and punish: (1) the exclusive right to make laws that may be enforced by means of punishment and that those within the territory of the political society over which it claims dominion are (at least typically) morally obliged to obey, and (2) the exclusive right to enforce these laws by means of punishment.[2]

A thesis which I call *political voluntarism* offers the following answer to the question with which this chapter began:

---

[1] This definition is meant to encompass a federal government of interlocking parts joined together by relations of cooperation and hierarchy. These parts collectively possess a monopoly on the power to legislate, and on the power to punish, even though no one part possesses a monopoly on the power to legislate or the power to punish. There is a sense in which two warring factions vying for control of a single territory also collectively possess a monopoly on the powers to legislate and to punish. But one would not want to call the sum of these warring factions a single government. Certain relations of cooperation and coordination must exist among the various parts for them jointly to constitute a government.

[2] Cf. Locke, II. 3, II. 87–8. A. John Simmons offers a similar formulation of the Lockean account of legitimacy in Simmons, 'Justification and Legitimacy', *Ethics*, 109 (1999): 739–71, at 746, and Simmons, 'On the Territorial Rights of States', *Philosophical Issues*, 35 (2001) (supplement to *Noûs*): 300–26.

An individual is subject to the legitimate political authority of a government if and only if, and by virtue of the fact that, he has given his free, rational, and informed consent to this subjection.[3]

It is a consequence of this thesis that a legitimately governed political society is a *voluntary association* in the following respect: an entire group of individuals in a given territory is subject to the legitimate political authority of a government if and only if each member of that group has given his free, rational, and informed consent to this subjection.

A political voluntarist who insists that one's freely given express consent is a necessary condition of subjection to the legitimate authority of a government must immediately confront the following problem. It seems, on this account, too easy for individuals to dodge the authority of any government, since they can do so simply by withholding any positive avowal of allegiance. Only anarchists and their near relations are likely to be very attracted to a philosophy that bases legitimate political authority on freely given express consent.

Locke is a political voluntarist, since he affirms that one's free,[4] rational,[5] and informed[6] consent is both a necessary[7] and a sufficient[8]

---

[3] (i) Note that this formulation employs the phrase 'has given ... consent' rather than 'would give ... consent'. The consent in question is actual rather than hypothetical. (ii) I endorse Joseph Raz's proposal that consent to be governed should be understood as 'roughly equivalent to the performative sense of "agreement"' (i.e. 'entering into an agreement to'), where the performative sense is to be contrasted with the 'cognitive' sense, which involves being of like mind (i.e. 'being in agreement that') (see Raz, *The Morality of Freedom* (Oxford: Oxford University Press, 1986), 80–1). As I shall explain in Section I below, in Locke's case consent consists of an agreement of the following sort: an agreement to transfer certain rights that one possesses in a state of nature.

[4] See II. 192. He also refers to such consent as voluntary in (e.g.) II. 173.

[5] See II. 131.

[6] Though Locke never explicitly says in the *Second Treatise* that such consent must be informed, he could not have thought otherwise, given the moral significance he attributes to knowledge of the laws, duties, and authorities that bind one (see II. 57, II. 59, II. 60, II. 63, II. 124–5, II. 131, II. 135–7, II. 170).

[7] In II. 95, for example, he asserts that 'no one can be ... subjected to the political power of another, without his own consent'. Locke believes, however, that a government could come to have legitimate 'despotical' power over those who 'forfeit' their natural rights by committing certain injustices (II. 172–3, II. 196). In so far as forfeiture is the result of a free choice to do wrong, there is a limited sense in which those who are under the despotical authority of government through forfeiture are freely under that authority. Unlike one who is placed under inescapable authority by birth or conquest, they could have chosen a different fate for themselves. Yet their forfeiture-inducing choice was not a choice to subject themselves to the authority of government, and therefore they, unlike consenters, are unwillingly subjected. These individuals are subject to specifically *despotical* rather than political authority, so, at least technically speaking, their subjection does not constitute a qualification to the claim that consent is a necessary condition of subjection to legitimate *political* authority.

[8] In II. 119 Locke asserts that 'No body doubts but an express *consent*, of any man entering into any society, makes him a perfect member of that society, a subject of that government'. By

condition of subjection to the legitimate political authority of a government. Locke's brand of voluntarism is immune to the afore-mentioned threat of anarchy, since on his account individuals tacitly consent to the authority of a government simply by remaining within the boundaries of the territory over which the government has domin-ion (II. 119).[9] But by allowing political authority to get a grip via tacit consent, Locke appears to fall into the opposite trap of making politi-cal authority too difficult to avoid. Lockean tacit consent has often been criticized on the ground that it is not genuinely free in the light of the economic and cultural costs of withholding one's consent in the only way possible: by leaving the political society in which one lives.[10] This is the first of two familiar criticisms of the claim that such con-sent is a sufficient condition of subjection to the legitimate authority of a government. The second is that such consent is not forthcoming against a background of equality and is hence tainted by the unequal bargaining power of the contracting parties.[11] My left-libertarian reconstruction of Locke's theory of legitimate political authority will be informed by the aim of overcoming both of these problems with his account of tacit consent.[12] It will build on my egalitarian

such consent one becomes a member of political society and a subject of its government on terms which are perpetual and indispensable (II. 121). Tacit consent, by contrast, is sufficient to make one neither a member of political society nor perpetually or indispensably a subject (II. 122). But it is a sufficient condition of subjection to legitimate political authority for as long as one owns land or resides or moves within the governed territory (II. 119). Simmons claims that Locke else-where denies that free, rational, and informed consent is sufficient to ground an obligation to obey a government. He cites II. 134, where Locke notes that an oath of obedience to a govern-ment would not bind if this would come into conflict with a consensual obligation of obedience to another government that one has already incurred. Simmons maintains, more generally, that 'consent cannot bind us where it exceeds our rights to give it' and cites 'consent to . . . subject ourselves to the political slavery of absolute, arbitrary government' as an example (Simmons, *On the Edge of Anarchy* (Princeton, NJ: Princeton University Press, 1993), 209). In contrast to Simmons, I believe Locke would deem it impossible to offer one's consent at all in these cases and hence I do not regard them as counter examples to the claim that Locke affirms that free, rational, and informed consent is a sufficient condition of obedience. For an explanation of why I think he would deem it impossible, see the third from last paragraph of Ch. 6 Sect. I below.

[9] In Section II below, I explain how, for Locke, a government acquires dominion over a ter-ritory.

[10] See David Hume, 'Of the Original Contract', in his *Essays: Moral, Political, and Literary*, ed. T. H. Green and T. H. Grose (London: Longmans, 1882), i. 451. See also John Rawls, *Political Liberalism* (New York: Columbia University Press, 1993), 221–2, 277.

[11] See Rawls, *Political Liberalism*, 286–8, and Rawls, *Justice as Fairness: A Restatement* (Cambridge, Mass.: Harvard University Press, 2001), 52–5.

[12] A third familiar criticism of tacit consent via residence, also traceable to Hume's 'Of the Original Contract', can be dealt with more briefly in this footnote. This is the criticism that (*a*) individuals are unaware that governments construe residence as constituting tacit consent and (*b*) an individual's residence cannot constitute genuinely morally binding tacit consent if he is unaware that it is supposed to constitute such consent. Even if (*b*) is true, governments can easily overcome this difficulty by publicizing the fact that residence will be construed as

interpretation in Chapter 1 of the Lockean principle of justice in acquisition of worldly resources and will emerge from an exposition of Locke's unreconstructed account of political authority, to which I now turn.[13]

I

Locke affirms that each person upon reaching the age of majority finds himself in 'a *state of perfect freedom*' (II. 4), which implies, among other things, that he possesses natural rights to legislate and punish for the purpose of upholding the law of nature.[14] He holds that the government of a political society could acquire a monopoly on such rights to legislate and punish just in case each governed individual gives them up by means of free, rational, and informed consent to transfer these rights to the collective that constitutes the membership of political society, which thereupon entrusts these rights to the government.[15] Governments may also come to possess legitimate powers which extend beyond the codification and enforcement of the law of nature. These powers are derived from the free, rational, and informed consent of each individual to transfer, in addition to the above rights to legislate and punish, some of the rights of self- and world-ownership that he possesses in a state of nature. In so doing, he agrees to submit to the regulation of his behaviour by the laws of this society which 'in many things confine the liberty he had by the law of nature' (II. 129).[16] The legitimate authority of government consists of nothing more or

constituting tacit consent. I shall assume throughout this discussion that governments will have publicized this fact.

[13] In reconstructing Locke's theory I will not follow him in insisting that express consent is a necessary condition of membership in political society. On the account of tacit consent I will offer, such tacit consent could be sufficient to make one a member of a political society rather than merely a subject of its government. I will also depart from Locke's claim that membership in political society is to be understood as perpetual and indispensable. I grant that there are circumstances in which a political society might legitimately offer only perpetual and indispensable membership. But I see neither reason to preclude a political society from offering non-permanent and dispensable membership nor reason to deny that an individual could consensually bind himself to such terms (see n. 8 above).

[14] See Ch. 3 above for a fuller discussion of these claims.

[15] See II. 22, II. 87, II. 95, II. 134, II. 136.

[16] Zoning laws and other forms of town and city planning provide an illustration of these powers which extend beyond the codification and enforcement of the law of nature. It is not a law of nature that the development of towns and cities be regulated to ensure sufficient open spaces and architectural harmony. But individuals could empower the government to impose these regulations by consensually transferring those property rights they possess in a state of nature that would otherwise stand in the way of the government's imposing these regulations.

less than the sum of the above rights that it acquires by means of the consensual transfer of these rights from individuals in a state of nature (II. 135).

Locke is mindful of the many practical problems that would accompany his admittedly 'strange doctrine' that individuals in a state of nature possess rights to legislate and punish for the purpose of upholding the law of nature.[17] Regarding the right to punish, Locke notes that 'I doubt not but it will be objected, that it is unreasonable for men to be judges in their own cases, that self-love will make men partial to themselves and their friends: and on the other side, that ill nature, passion and revenge will carry them too far in punishing others; and hence nothing but confusion and disorder will follow' (II. 13).[18] Such confusion and disorder would arise out of disagreement over the propriety of verdicts and sentences in particular cases even if everyone shared the same general opinion of what types of acts are punishable and to what degree—even if, in other words, everyone legislated in the same manner. If, however, legislating individuals were to come to conflicting opinions regarding the justifiability of attaching punishments of various degrees to the commission of various acts, this would multiply the sources of discord. One could therefore point to similar problems with the exercise of the right of each to legislate and the consequent absence of a governmental monopoly on the power to create 'an *established*, settled, known *law*' which is 'the standard of right and wrong, and the common measure to decide all controversies between them' (II. 124).[19] These difficulties would be especially pronounced among individuals who live and intermingle within the confines of a community such as a village or town.[20]

The aforementioned difficulties with the right of each to legislate and punish in order to uphold the law of nature are, I think, sufficient to establish the following obligation on the part of individuals for the sake of peace and security: an obligation to relinquish these rights to

[17] He describes this 'doctrine' as 'strange' in II. 13.　　　　[18] See also II. 125–6.

[19] Critics of Locke contend that such practical considerations tell decisively against Locke's tenet that adults possess natural rights to legislate and punish. (See, for example, Elizabeth Anscombe, 'On the Source of the Authority of the State', in her *Collected Philosophical Papers of G. E. M. Anscombe*, iii. *Ethics, Religion, and Politics* (Minneapolis, Minn.: University of Minnesota Press, 1981), 148–9.) But Locke does not believe that these problems are sufficient to refute the claim that adults possess natural rights to legislate and punish, nor does he think that they provide a justification for forcing persons to join political societies in the absence of their consent. There is, for him, another means—tacit consent—of reconciling the requirement of consent with the need for order that justifies a governmental monopoly on the powers to legislate and punish within a given stretch of territory. I shall say more about Lockean tacit consent in Sections II–V below.

[20] '[G]overnment is hardly to be avoided amongst men that live together' (II. 105).

legislate and punish and instead to place themselves under a competent and effective common government whenever they live, intermingle, and interact with others within the confines of a community that is much larger or more complex than a hamlet.[21]

The aforementioned difficulties would, however, be largely absent in the case of isolated persons who live—and in so far as they remain—within the boundaries of clearly defined territories that they legitimately own and that lie beyond the boundaries of such communities. Hence, it is far less clear that an obligation to relinquish natural rights to legislate and punish reaches such isolated individuals. A Lockean could understand the natural rights of individuals to legislate and punish not as rights to intermingle with others as so many roving governors who exercise powers of legislation and punishment as they each see fit over all in their sights, but rather as rights of each to govern a discrete and isolated bit of territory. When such rights are so understood, the case for rights of individuals in a state of nature to legislate and punish will begin to look less strange.

Even when we limit ourselves to territorially bounded rights to legislate and punish, the opportunity will inevitably arise for disputes about and across borders between individuals who govern their own territory and others who live beyond the borders of this territory. But it does not immediately follow from this fact that, rather than submit to neutral and impartial arbitration of these disputes, these others have the right to bring these individuals within their governance. If this right did follow, then such reasoning would seem equally to rule out a plurality of the more familiar sort of separate and sovereign territorially bounded states that might come into conflict with one another. Citing difficulties similar to those that Locke notes, Jeremy Waldron has argued that 'I should enter quickly into a form of society with those immediately adjacent to me, those with whose interests my resource use is likely to pose the most frequent and dangerous conflicts'.[22] This principle, while falling short of implying one world government, appears to have the striking consequence that a plurality of independent states should not exist if some of their members live in close proximity to the members of an adjacent state. Since only island

---

[21] Simmons has convincingly argued that Locke denies an *unconditional* obligation to relinquish private rights to legislate and punish and enter into political society (see Simmons, *The Lockean Theory of Rights* (Princeton, NJ: Princeton University Press, 1992), 66–7). But Simmons's textual evidence is consistent with an obligation to relinquish private rights to legislate and punish *if* one chooses to live, intermingle, and interact with others within the confines of a community.

[22] Jeremy Waldron, 'Special Ties and Natural Duties', *Philosophy and Public Affairs*, 22 (1993): 3–30, at 15.

states and those with uninhabited frontiers would pass muster, few of the intracontinental political divisions would withstand this test of legitimacy. But since such intracontinental political divisions are in fact feasible even when they involve multiple subdivisions (including those in Europe that carve out such tiny states as Liechtenstein, Andorra, San Marino, Monaco, and the Vatican City), one should not be too hasty in rejecting territorially bounded rights of individuals to legislate and punish on grounds of practical impossibility.[23]

II

The possibility of territorially bounded rights of individuals to legislate and punish opens an interesting path—which I explore in this section—toward a defence of the Lockean voluntarist's claim that the free, rational, and informed consent of the governed is sufficient to legitimate the authority of their government.

This exploration begins with the observation that private rights over land in a state of nature imply certain territorially bounded rights to legislate and punish. This is because the right to private property carries with it the right to exclude others from one's estate or to permit their entry on to one's estate only on terms that one has chosen. These terms might be regarded as the laws of one's estate which one had the right to decree, and also to enforce at least by means of expulsion from one's property, by virtue of one's right of ownership of that estate and the power to exclude and include that this carries.[24] These laws may go beyond the mere enforcement of, though they cannot contradict, the law of nature. One could acquire a monopoly over all rights to legislate and punish on one's estate by setting as a condition of others' entry on to one's estate their agreement to relinquish their rights to legislate and punish therein.

A government, according to Locke, comes to have dominion over land when private individuals transfer certain of their property rights in their land to this government (II. 120). As one interpreter of Locke explains:

[23] I shall return in Section VI below to the problem that disputes about and across borders in a state of nature pose for Lockeans. But in the intervening Sections II–V I shall offer an idealized account of the rise of legitimate political authority which assumes the absence of such disputes.

[24] Textual evidence of such a territorially bounded understanding of rights to legislate and punish can be found in II. 122, where Locke speaks of the laws and government of a head of a family which would apply to an outsider who found it convenient to abide with this family for some time. Evidence can also be found in II. 123, where Locke speaks of 'man in the state of nature' as 'absolute lord of his own person and possessions', which he refers to as his 'empire'.

The [landowning] founders [of a political society] mutually agreed to restrict their rights in their land in various ways designed to insure that anyone who came on the land would be obligated to obey the government's laws. Perhaps they promised neither to violate, nor to permit others to violate, the laws while on their land; more importantly, they transferred to the government the right to demand the compliance of anyone else who comes upon the land.[25]

They could bring about the latter by transferring to the government a subset of their rights to permit the entry of others on to their estates. More precisely, they could transfer to the government their right to permit the entry of those who have not consented to transfer their natural rights to legislate and punish to the government and to obey the laws of the government. The government would thereby be entitled to bar anybody who did not consent to its authority from entering or remaining on this territory. It could exercise this entitlement by publicly declaring that an individual may enter or remain upon this territory only on condition that he thereby tacitly consent to transfer his rights to legislate and punish to this government and to obey the government's laws for the duration that he remains within the boundaries of this territory.[26] According to Locke, such tacit consent would, if free, rational, and informed, be morally binding so long as the laws that the consenter has agreed to obey do not violate the law of nature. This consent would, he thinks, be free even if it were very difficult or even impossible to uproot and find a place to live outside the boundaries of the governed territory.

David Hume famously complains, against Locke's account of tacit consent, that saying that 'a poor peasant or artisan has a free choice to leave his country when he knows no foreign language or manners, and lives from day to day, by the small wages which he acquires' is akin to saying 'that a man, by remaining in a vessel, freely consents to the dominion of the master; though he was carried on board while asleep, and must leap into the ocean, and perish, the moment he leaves her'.[27] Under a familiar interpretation of this passage, Hume takes his example to be an illustration of the following pair of claims: if it is very difficult or costly to avoid doing that which is alleged to constitute tacit consent, then the consent is not free; moreover, consent must be free in order to be morally binding.[28]

---

[25]   Charles Beitz, 'Tacit Consent and Property Rights', *Political Theory*, 8 (1980): 487–502, at 492–3.

[26]   Such a public declaration would meet the criticism of Lockean tacit consent mentioned in Ch. 5 n. 12 above.

[27]   Hume, 'Of the Original Contract', 451.

[28]   Simmons, for example, offers this interpretation in Simmons, *On the Edge of Anarchy*, 233. It is not, however, obvious from the text that Hume affirms the above pair of claims.

One might question whether consent must, in order to be morally binding, be free in the sense of being not very difficult or costly to avoid.[29] It is, after all, very costly because lethal for someone to refrain from consenting to pay a surgeon the fee that she requires to perform a live-saving operation. Yet such consent, when informed, could be sufficient to render the patient liable to pay the surgeon this fee.[30] It does not matter whether the consent to pay the fee is express (as is typically the case) or tacit (as it would be if the surgeon declared to a competent adult who is fully capable of doing so that failure to get up and walk away from the operating table constitutes consent to pay the fee). In either case, it could be morally binding.

In spite of these observations, Hume's complaint nevertheless carries force. Even if one concedes that consent that is unfree in so far as it is very difficult or costly to withhold could be morally binding, unfree consent is inferior to free consent in so far as it lacks an additional, powerful rationale that free consent supplies for the imposition of the terms of the agreement upon the consenting individual. Free consent alone provides the following rationale for such imposition: since this individual could, without great cost or difficulty, have walked away from these terms but nevertheless chose to accept them, he does not have recourse to the complaint that he was forced either by circumstances or by others to accept them. The difference in the

[29] Throughout this section 'free consent' should be understood as 'consent that is not very difficult or costly to avoid'. (In Sect. V I shall consider a different construal of 'free consent' which identifies it with 'voluntary (i.e. willing) consent'.) I should note that Locke himself could hardly have believed that consent was free just in case it was not very difficult or costly to avoid. He claims that tacit consent by means of continued residence is sufficient to oblige one to obey the government for the duration of one's residence and hence that it is free. Yet surely he was aware that such consent was very difficult or costly for many to avoid. Locke maintains that consent could not bind if it was 'extorted by force' (II. 186). Yet his explanation (ibid.) of why such consent does not bind appeals to the fact that it was secured by means that run contrary to the natural law. It does not appeal to the fact that such consent was very difficult or costly to avoid. Elsewhere, Locke declares that 'a Man can no more justly make use of another's necessity, to force him to become his Vassal, by with-holding that Relief, God requires him to afford to the wants of his Brother, than he that has more strength can seize upon a weaker, master him to his Obedience, and with a Dagger at his Throat offer him Death or Slavery' (Locke, *Two Treatises of Government*, ed. Peter Laslett (Cambridge: Cambridge University Press, 1988), bk. I, §42). Here again Locke could appeal to the fact that consent that was secured by means of withholding relief that one owes does not bind because it was secured by means that run contrary to the natural law.

[30] Interestingly, this example is in fact Hume's: 'A man, dangerously wounded, who promises a competent sum to a surgeon to cure him, wou'd certainly be bound to performance' (Hume, *A Treatise of Human Nature*, ed. David Norton and Mary Norton (Oxford: Oxford University Press, 2000), bk. III, pt. II, sect. v). This passage from Hume casts doubt on the soundness of what I have called the 'familiar interpretation' of Hume's 'poor peasant or artisan' passage, since one could render the 'surgeon' passage consistent with the 'poor peasant or artisan' passage only if one abandoned the familiar interpretation of the latter.

justificatory force of free versus unfree consent is revealed by the following pair of cases. In the first, the only surgeon in town charges a fee far above her reservation price (i.e. the minimum fee for which she'd be willing to work) for a life-saving operation. In the second, this surgeon charges a fee far above her reservation price for inessential cosmetic surgery. A patient's informed consent to pay the high fee would uncontroversially oblige him to do so in the second case but not in the first. This is because unfree consent can bind only to terms that are reasonable.[31] The same is not true of free consent.

Locke opens himself up to Hume's complaint because he accepts, as a just consequence of the introduction of money, the emergence of an inegalitarian division of the population into landowners and landless workers. Moreover, he believes that these landowners could ensure that land remain under the government of a political society in perpetuity by irrevocably transferring the right to govern this land to this government (II. 73, II. 117). Since this transfer would be irrevocable, anyone who purchases or inherits this land would be subject to similar restrictions that ensure that anyone who occupies this land is under the government of the political society. Hence, a single generation of individuals who jointly own all available land could, by such transfer, ensure that all subsequent generations be confronted with the choice between treading international-ocean water and tacitly consenting to subjection to the government of one or another political society as a consequence of setting foot on any land at all.

I have argued in Chapter 1 that this inegalitarianism in Locke is indefensible. It is inconsistent with a proper understanding of the conditions under which individuals may justifiably come to own previously unowned worldly resources. Contrary to Locke's own understanding of these conditions, they call for an egalitarian pattern of ownership of land and other worldly resources among the members of each generation. On my understanding of these conditions, each member of the first generation to confront an expanse of previously unowned territory could legitimately acquire worldly resources just in case this acquisition is consistent with the possibility of every other member of that generation's coming to own worldly resources that are

---

[31] But it does not follow that such unfree consent is morally superfluous. Even if a patient's consent to pay a specified reasonable fee for a life-saving operation is unfree because it can be withheld only at the cost of death, such consent would serve to bind him to that fee rather than a different fee which the surgeon could reasonably have charged instead. Moreover, if a competent adult withheld consent both to pay a reasonable fee and to undergo a life-saving operation (which, let us assume, involves a relatively safe and painless procedure), it would be unjust in the absence of his consent to force him to undergo such an operation and to pay a reasonable fee.

equally advantageous. One person's resources are as advantageous as another's just in case they enable that person to improve his situation to the same degree as the other, as measured in terms of their opportunities for welfare. Acquisition of previously unowned resources on these terms is 'no prejudice to any other' (II. 33). Moreover, individuals would reasonably be required not just to ensure that no members of their own generation are placed at a disadvantage, but also to ensure the same opportunities of ownership for members of subsequent generations. Contrary to Locke, the advent of money and the practice of bequests cannot supersede the requirement that one leave 'enough and as good' and therefore cannot give rise to a state of affairs in which some are left without any claim of ownership over land and other worldly resources upon reaching majority.

Under such an egalitarian principle of ownership of worldly resources, an autonomous and sovereign political society in the form of a city, town, or village that occupies a continuous stretch of territory could arise through the banding together of a number of individuals and their placing under collective governance the contiguous plots of land that they have acquired in the state of nature. This political society would be akin to 'a quilt patched together from individual holdings in land'.[32] Let us concede, for the reasons given in Section I above, that if individuals choose to enter into or remain in a territorially bounded political society such as a city, town, or village then they must relinquish their rights of self-governance to a government that enjoys a monopoly on the rights to legislate and punish within the boundaries of this political society. The members of a city, town, or village could legitimately prevent the rise of independently governed enclaves within their political society by preventing the acquisition of land within their boundaries by those who refuse to agree to submit this land to collective governance. This they would be entitled to do so long as they manage to leave 'enough and as good' so that unconsenting individuals are able to acquire unowned land, or have sufficient resources to purchase owned land, beyond the boundaries of their political society. By leaving 'enough and as good' they would ensure that their establishment of such a political society 'injures not the freedom of the rest' (II. 95). Given an egalitarian reading of the 'enough-and-as-good' proviso, any individual who chooses not to submit to the authority of the government of any political society would retain the opportunity to acquire or purchase a plot of land beyond these

---

[32] Beitz, 'Tacit Consent and Property Rights', 493.

boundaries and declare it a 'monity' governed by laws of his own making and of which he is the sole enforcer.[33]

If people wish to form political societies that extend beyond the boundaries of a single city, town, or village and more closely resemble the far greater reach of modern-day states, they might attempt to create such a commonwealth through the patching together of a great many contiguous, privately owned plots of land into a single large territory. This territory would encompass cities, towns, or villages and the less densely populated spaces between these communities. If this commonwealth were large enough, it is unlikely that its members could justifiably demand, as a condition on acquisition of territory anywhere within this commonwealth by those who were born, raised, and have attained majority therein, the submission of this plot of land to the collective governance of this commonwealth. This is because it is doubtful that the choice between such submission and withdrawal beyond the outer boundaries of such a large commonwealth would leave 'enough and as good' for unconsenting individuals. Rather, the satisfaction of the 'enough-and-as-good' proviso would probably require the provision of opportunities for each individual in this territory who wishes not to submit to the government of any political society to acquire or purchase a plot of land in the less densely populated areas within the boundaries of the commonwealth but beyond the boundaries of its cities, towns, and villages and declare this plot a sovereign entity governed by laws of his own making and of which he is the sole enforcer: a right of the individual to internal secession.[34]

Given the rights of world-ownership and secession that I have sketched in this section, the Humean complaint regarding the unfreedom of tacit consent loses some of its edge, since each unconsenting individual would have the option of withdrawing not into the ocean, but into the plot of land which he would have the opportunity to acquire or purchase under the correct egalitarian principles of justice in acquisition and which he would be entitled to declare a sovereign and independent entity. Moreover, the egalitarian nature of the prin-

---

[33] 'Monity' is a term I hereby coin to refer to a political 'society' of one: a single individual in a given territory who is the sole governor of this territory and who, in the absence of guests, is also the sole inhabitant of this territory. Monities and political societies are types of polity.

[34] Leaving aside their threats of violence, acts of fraud, racism, anti-Semitism, and apparently unjust occupation of someone else's land, perhaps the actions of the Montana Freemen were not as crazy as one might think. There might be respectable Lockean grounds for the right of secession that they affirmed. The beliefs and activities of the Freemen are described in Dale and Connie Jakes, *False Prophets: The Firsthand Account of a Husband–Wife Team Working for the FBI and Living in Deepest Cover with the Montana Freemen* (Los Angeles, Calif.: NewStar Media, 1998).

ciple of world-ownership that I endorse addresses the second complaint against Lockean voluntarism to which I referred at the beginning of this chapter: the complaint that Lockean consent is not forthcoming against a background of equality and is hence tainted by the unequal bargaining power of the contracting parties.[35]

III

An individual who lives alone on a self-governed plot of land may lack the benefits which others in political society enjoy of communal relations and of economies of scale stemming from the collectivization of land.[36] Who should bear the cost of these disadvantages of living alone: the lone individual or the community? In other words, when, if ever, does an individual have a claim of compensation from the community for these disadvantages? The answer to this question bears crucially on the nature of an individual's right to live free of the bonds of political society on a self-governed plot of land, where this right is supposed to help legitimate the tacit consent via residence of those who choose to live within the boundaries of a political society. My answer to this question is dictated by the logic of the principle of equality of opportunity for welfare according to which an individual

[35] If I am right to condemn Locke's own understanding of the principles governing justice in acquisition of worldly resources as unjustifiably inegalitarian, then his account of tacit consent is open to a further objection that is distinct from the above two objections. This objection is also met by an egalitarian distribution of worldly resources. Individuals who acquire land in accordance with Locke's indefensibly inegalitarian, rather than a properly egalitarian, interpretation of the proviso would possess illegitimate claims to more than their fair share of land. So also would any collective government under whose jurisdiction these individuals place this land. This illegitimacy would in itself be sufficient to refute the claim that residing within this territory constitutes tacit consent to the authority of those who govern it. It would be sufficient even if it were not costly to leave such governed territory and even if this inequality in land ownership would not give rise to inequalities in bargaining powers among the contracting parties. To see why this is so, consider the following analogy: Imagine that you and I each rightfully owns an equally large estate. Suppose that you declare that my walking on some part of *my own estate*, say its remote south-west corner, constitutes tacit consent to abide by a code of conduct that you have drawn up. It would not follow that my walking on this remote part of my large estate constitutes any such tacit consent. This would not follow even if it were of little cost for me to avoid the south-west corner of my large estate and even in the absence of any inequalities in our bargaining power. It would not follow for the simple reason that this land is not under your proper jurisdiction. The same would hold if you had illegitimately annexed the south-west corner of my estate. It would also hold if you had unjustly appropriated this patch of land out of an original unowned state in violation of the egalitarian proviso.

[36] When people live alone rather than in society there will also be greater costs associated with policing and adjudicating disputes and providing protection.

must bear the cost of voluntarily chosen disadvantage whereas society must bear the cost of unchosen disadvantage.[37]

Let us first consider cases involving a lone individual and a single political society. If, on the one hand, the lone individual's outsider status is the result of involuntary exclusion, then the community which excludes him should compensate him for the disadvantages of living alone.[38] Suppose, on the other hand, that an individual's outsider status is the result of a voluntary choice to be outside even though he has the option of membership in political society. In this case, if the option of membership into political society was offered on terms that provide him with less opportunity for welfare than others or are otherwise unreasonable by his own lights, then those who offered these terms should bear the losses. They don't, simply by offering him a choice of membership, no matter how unfavourable the terms, thereby transfer responsibility to bear the losses on to him. But if the membership was offered on terms that provide him with opportunity for welfare that is equal to that of others and are otherwise reasonable by his own lights, then he should bear these losses. This individual would still be entitled to a self-governed plot of land which would, roughly speaking, be equivalent in value to a $1/n$ share of the world, where 'n' represents the number of inhabitants in the world. But he would not be entitled to compensation for lack of community or non-collectivization of resources.[39]

We can generalize from the above to cases involving lone individuals who choose to remain outside *multiple* political societies. Suppose that at least one of those societies offers a lone individual membership on terms that provide him with opportunity for welfare that is equal to that of others and are otherwise reasonable by his own lights. In this case, other political societies that exclude him do not owe him any compensation. Nor, then, is compensation owed by political societies that offer him terms that provide him with less opportunity for welfare than others or are otherwise unreasonable by his own lights. If, however, no society offers him membership on terms that provide him

[37] See Ch. 1 Sect. III above.

[38] In saying that the community is liable to compensate an individual for excluding him from society, I depart from Locke's position on this matter as sketched in II. 95. There he says that 'any number of men may' enter into an agreement 'to join and unite into a community' because this 'injures not the freedom of the rest; they are left as they were in the liberty of the state of nature'.

[39] I say 'roughly speaking' because, on my welfare-egalitarian reading of the Lockean proviso, the size of this share would, strictly speaking, need to be adjusted in order to compensate for differences in individuals' abilities to convert worldly resources into welfare. Such adjustments would need to be made even though here we refrain from compensating for those differences in welfare which arise from the benefits stemming from community with others and the collectivization of resources in political society.

with opportunity for welfare that is equal to that of others and are otherwise reasonable by his own lights, then he is owed compensation whose cost must be shared by all of the other political societies, whether they excluded him or offered him terms that provide him with less opportunity for welfare than others or are otherwise unreasonable by his own lights. In the light of this, we can see that the more—and more varied the range of—political societies which it might be possible for an individual to join, the more likely that the onus will be on the individual to bear the losses of living alone. I shall have more to say regarding the virtues of such pluralism in the next section.

IV

The alternative to being a member of any political society which is supposed to underpin morally binding tacit consent via residence is the option of withdrawing into a self-governed plot of land to which one would be entitled by the Lockean principle of justice in acquisition. This alternative reduces but does not eliminate the force of Hume's objection to tacit consent via residence. A serious problem remains, which I shall address in this section.

For certain rugged individualists the option of living in isolation from others on a self-governed plot of land will be sufficient to provide an attractive alternative to life in political society even in the absence of monetary compensation for the lack of goods of community. But for many individuals no sum of worldly resources would render life in isolation outside political society nearly as good as life in political society under ordinary circumstances. It would always be possible through monetary transfers from the members of political society to those outside political society to make life in political society as dire as life in isolation.[40] But it would often be impossible to make life in isolation nearly as good as life in political society under ordinary and attractive circumstances.

For those for whom this would be impossible the alternative of life outside any political society would not in itself be sufficient to justify the claim that residence within the boundaries of a given political

---

[40] In extreme cases this would involve a transfer from the members of the community to isolated outsiders which is so great that the immiseration of the members of this community would render them no better off than the compensated outsider. Such a point would eventually be reached, since sufficient transfers of resources would eventually result in misery to the members of this community from hunger, dehydration, and exposure to the elements.

society constitutes morally binding tacit consent to its government. In their case, the following would typically be necessary in order to justify an inference of morally binding tacit consent from the fact of residence in a given political society. It would be necessary that these individuals have a diverse range of choices of political societies which occupy the full range of political, cultural, and urban-to-rural possibilities to which people tend to be attracted. It would also be necessary that they possess the material resources to flourish in any of a range of these societies and to easily relocate from one to another. In such circumstances, it would be justifiable to infer from the choices of individuals to remain within the borders of a given political society rather than any of the others that they genuinely consent to the authority of the government of this society. We can infer that it is not simply out of resignation, in the face of a paucity of choice, that they remain in this one rather than another, but rather because they were able, given the diverse range of possibilities, to live in a community which suits them well.[41]

Such a decision to remain within the borders of a given political society might be regarded as especially indicative of free choice rather than mere accommodation in the case of those who have not formed familial ties involving long-term partners and dependent children.[42] In the case of those who have formed such ties, even substantial wealth and a diverse range of nearby political societies might not provide the individual with a genuine choice of political societies. Relocation might require the severing of these ties. Even if it would not, there might not be a single political society amidst this diversity which every member of this family could wholeheartedly embrace, given their conflicting needs and preferences and different occupational opportunities. If morally binding consent is to be inferred from residence, then

[41] As I shall explain in Section V below, someone who finds life outside political society intolerable might offer his morally binding tacit consent via residence even in the absence of such a range of options. But we would, in the absence of further information, not be epistemically justified in inferring consent from such residence.

[42] Consider the case of the actual range of choice of university community—and therefore home for the next four years—that is open to a reasonably well off, academically high-achieving, 18-year-old American who is free of such ties. He is able to choose among large state universities or small liberal-arts colleges, academically excellent Ivy League institutions or those which place a greater emphasis on social or athletic endeavours, institutions with socially liberal or traditionally conservative reputations, religious or secular institutions, places in the middle of nowhere or in the midst of a metropolis, the local university or institutions in a different region of the country or another country in a different part of the world. Even if he had no acceptable alternative to going to some college or university, his attending one of them versus any of a range of others could be regarded as providing the grounds for the attribution of genuine consent to the rules of that institution when the feasible set of colleges or universities among which he chose was sufficiently rich.

it is especially important, in the light of these complications, that people have an adequate range of choices, and the wherewithal to make these choices, in their early years of adulthood when they will be more likely to be able to take full advantage of these options.[43]

Under what conditions would one find nearby diversity of political societies and the material wherewithal to choose among them? A distribution of resources in accordance with the egalitarian proviso would tend to provide individuals with the wherewithal to flourish in any of a number of different societies and to move from one to another. But an egalitarian distribution of resources would not in itself be sufficient to ensure the diversity of political societies. Additional measures involving the decentralization of political authority and the fostering of local autonomy would need to be taken in order to realize this. A pluralistic confederation of political societies on the small scale of autonomous cities, towns, and regions would be more likely to provide such a diversity of choice than political societies on a larger scale in which the laws and institutions are fairly uniform throughout, even if they are uniformly liberal throughout. In the following chapter, I shall sharpen the contrast I have just drawn and offer a defence of such pluralism in the face of some of its more extreme consequences.

V

In Section II above, I construed Hume as arguing, by means of his example of the person brought on board the ship, that residence within a political society constitutes free and morally binding consent to the authority of the government of that society only if it is not very difficult or costly to live outside this society. I noted that while Hume's own example of the surgeon casts serious doubt on the claim that this is a necessary condition of morally binding consent, the presence of an attractive alternative to residence in a political society nevertheless lends support to the claim that such consent is morally binding. In this section I shall examine the conditions under which consent via residence would be morally binding even in the absence of any decent alternative to residence. I shall argue that even in the absence of any alternative at all such residence might constitute

---

[43] Even if they are provided with the diversity and the wherewithal to make a free choice at this young age, their circumstances might eventually change such that they must choose between the society they freely embrace and the person or persons with whom they want to live. This diversity and wherewithal does not provide a guarantee that individuals will be able, without great cost, to live in a society to which they freely consent.

consent that is free in the sense of being *voluntary*, where 'voluntary' here is understood as a synonym for 'willing'. Moreover, such consent might be morally binding.

Locke himself demonstrates, by means of an example in his *Essay concerning Human Understanding*, that one can willingly φ even if one has no alternative to φ-ing:

[S]uppose a man be carried, whilst fast asleep, into a room where is a person he longs to see and speak with; and be there locked fast in, beyond his power to get out: he awakes, and is glad to find himself in so desirable company, which he stays willingly in, i.e. prefers his stay to going away.... [Y]et, being locked fast in, it is evident he is not at liberty not to stay, he has not freedom to be gone.[44]

The same might be true of a person's residence within a given political society. Under relevantly similar conditions, even if it is impossible for you to leave that society you might nevertheless willingly remain within its boundaries. Now the mere fact that you prefer your 'stay to going away' is not enough to establish that your stay is willing. For you might prefer to remain within the confines of a kidnapper's damp cellar because you know that he will recapture and torture you the moment you escape. It is reasonable to maintain that such a preference does not render your remaining within the cellar willing. Even if it does, the willingness of your confinement would in no way constitute morally binding consent to this confinement. Even in the absence of rights-violating confinement and deterrence, a preference for staying rather than leaving is not enough to establish the willingness of the stay. For you might be driven by a flood to take refuge in the upper branches of a tree. You might cling to these branches because you prefer them to the dangers of the cold, swift currents below. Here it would be a stretch to claim that your stay in the upper reaches of this tree is willing. But even if we would be warranted in describing such a stay as willing, we should be reluctant to infer morally binding consent from such a stay. By parity of reasoning, we should be reluctant to infer that you consent in morally binding fashion to the authority of the hellish political society in which you reside if you reside therein simply because life outside political society is even more hellish. We should be reluctant to make such an inference even if nobody is responsible for the fact that life in this political society is hellish and life outside it even more hellish.

---

[44] Locke, *An Essay concerning Human Understanding*, ed. Peter Nidditch (Oxford: Oxford University Press, 1975), bk. 2, ch. 21, sect. 10.

Now suppose by contrast that the political society in which you reside is more than merely preferable to any alternative but also positively attractive to you in absolute terms. In this case it would be reasonable to infer that your remaining within the boundaries of this society is not merely willing but willing in a respect which grounds the claim that such residence constitutes morally binding consent to the authority of that society. This might be true even if you have no alternative to life in such a society. You might, as in the case of Locke's man in the locked room, find yourself in such desirable company in this political society, and you might find many other aspects of this political society so attractive, that it would be appropriate to conclude that you reside within the boundaries of this society because you wholeheartedly endorse its institutions, principles, and character. Here it would be legitimate to infer that your residence within the boundaries of this political society constitutes morally binding consent even though it is impossible for you to reside elsewhere.

In the light of these observations it is not strictly speaking necessary to provide individuals with the pluralistic choice of political societies which I sketched in the previous section in order to ensure that their residence within a given society constitutes morally binding consent where this consent is voluntary in the sense of willing. If each individual happens to find himself in the political society which he most prefers and which he also finds attractive in absolute terms, one could infer morally binding willing consent via residence in that society even if he had no alternative to life in that society. By analogy, even if several individuals at a restaurant are each provided with a menu that lists but a single dish, each person might wholeheartedly endorse his one choice if this dish happens to be his favourite. But we are, as a practical matter, much more justified in inferring that an individual wholeheartedly endorses the dish he has chosen if it has been chosen from a long and diverse menu of dishes which people tend to like. Similarly, we are, as a practical matter, much more justified in inferring that residence within a given political society constitutes morally binding willing consent if this political society is one of a diverse and readily accessible range of political societies that people tend to find attractive. Hence, good grounds can be provided for the decentralized, pluralistic, and open confederation of political societies which I sketched in the previous section even if we admit the possibility of morally binding willing consent in the absence of any alternatives.

VI

To this point I have artificially assumed the absence of disputes about and across the borders of political societies and monities.[45] In this concluding section, I shall explain how my account of legitimate political authority applies to more realistic circumstances in which such disputes exist.

In a Lockean state of nature disputes would undoubtedly arise over whether groups or individuals are entitled to stake claims to plots of land for the purpose of establishing autonomous and sovereign entities. Other sorts of conflicts among such a vast number of independent sovereignties would also need to be adjudicated. Indeed, the greater the number and diversity of autonomous cities, towns, and regions of the sort that I envisioned at the close of Section IV, the greater the likelihood of conflict. In the light of such difficulties, the closest one could actually come to a peaceful and orderly realization of the Lockean ideal of political societies as voluntary associations would be a fluid confederation of political societies and monities that is regulated by an interpolitical governing body.[46] It would be necessary for this governing body to possess limited powers which encompass the overseeing of the drawing of the boundaries that demarcate these societies and monities and the settling of disputes that might arise among these parties.[47] While the legitimate authority of the governments of the various societies would be based upon consent, the legitimate authority of this governing body would not necessarily be so based.[48] Given the disorder and chaos which would ensue in the absence of such a governing body, all individuals would legitimately be subject to its authority—even those who do not consent to it.[49] Hence, the ideal of political societies as voluntary associations would need to be underpinned by involuntary governance at the interpolitical level.[50] It does

[45] See n. 23 above.

[46] i.e. an overarching government body which regulates the relations between the various polities—political societies and monities—of this confederation.

[47] As I shall explain below, such an authority would also be needed to govern acquisition of worldly resources in accordance with the Lockean proviso more generally.

[48] Given this interpolitical governing body, those which I have just called the 'governments' of what I have just called '[political] societies' would not retain complete monopolies on the powers to legislate and punish. Therefore, given my definitions at the beginning of this chapter, we do not, strictly speaking, have 'governments' and 'political societies' here. But they are close enough to be so called.

[49] Perhaps disorder and chaos could be avoided if most but not all were subject to such authority. But fairness would rule out the subjection of some but not others who are similarly situated.

[50] See Thomas Christiano, *The Rule of the Many: Fundamental Issues in Democratic Theory* (Boulder, Colo.: Westview Press, 1996), 22–3.

not follow from the fact that involuntarism is justified at the inter-political level that this rationale carries over to justify involuntarism at the level of smaller political societies (and monities). The case for voluntarism is *overridden* by necessity at the interpolitical level even though it is not overridden by such considerations at the level of indi-vidual political societies. A voluntarist would be committed to the confinement of involuntary governance to the bare minimum neces-sary, given the moral undesirability of political authority in the absence of free consent. A voluntarist would also be committed to as democratic a means as possible of establishing and perpetuating such a governing body on the grounds that, other things being equal, the more democratic the means, the more closely such a body would approximate one that is based on unanimous consent.

It would be necessary for the limited powers of this governing body to encompass the adjudication of conflicts to which attempts to acquire plots of land and other worldly resources in a state of nature would give rise. The discord which Locke identifies as the conse-quence of the private exercise of the right to punish would arise as a consequence of the private exercise of the right to enforce one's claims over land and other resources in a state of nature. This would be true at least when we assume the sorts of competing claims on resources that would arise under conditions of even moderate scarcity. Hence, individuals would be obliged to place themselves under some form of common government to adjudicate disputes and enforce judgements as a condition of engaging in the acquisition of resources.

Disputes would, moreover, need to be adjudicated within the frame-work of something resembling 'an *established*, settled, known *law*' regarding justice in acquisition to serve as 'the standard of right and wrong, and the common measure to decide all controversies between them'. Individuals in a state of nature would need to conform to a common understanding of the proper application of the principles of justice in acquisition as set forth by the Lockean proviso. This is a demanding requirement. Even if, for example, individuals were all to unite around the egalitarian version of the proviso which I introduced in Chapter 1 Section III, that would still leave open the question of the appropriate metric of equality. Even if they were all to agree that this metric should be a welfarist one, that still leaves open the question of the particular conception of welfare to be adopted.

In agreeing upon the appropriate conception of welfare for the purpose of determining a fair division of worldly resources in accor-dance with the welfare-egalitarian proviso, individuals would need to be sensitive to the fact that reasonable people espouse a plurality of conflicting conceptions of what constitutes an individual's well-being. A follower of John Stuart Mill would claim that the correct conception of welfare for human beings places a premium on the 'higher pleasures' of intellectual and artistic activity and accord far less significance to the satisfaction of less rarefied sensual and materialistic urges. A libertine would reverse these priorities. Someone informed by a more spiritual outlook might downgrade the significance of both types of pleasure in favour of harmony with nature and contemplation of the divine. Irreconcilable conflicts would arise if individuals applied their differing conceptions to determine whether they are entitled, under the welfare-egalitarian proviso, to acquire any given unowned bit of the world. Individuals would need therefore to unite around a single conception of welfare in order to render the application of this proviso consistent. Each person would presumably favour his own conception on the grounds that it reveals the truth about well-being for human beings.[51] But people who espouse conflicting yet reasonable conceptions would have a legitimate complaint if one particular conception were adopted over others. They would therefore need to try to devise a conception of welfare which is sufficiently general to accommodate a plurality of more particular conceptions that reasonable people are likely to hold. This general conception should, in so far as possible, be neutral amongst these particular conceptions of welfare in the following respect: no one such conception should be presupposed as the right one to the exclusion of others for the purposes of determining when a distribution of worldly resources realizes equality of opportunity for welfare.

The following preference-based conception of welfare is ideally suited to this aim of neutrality: one which measures an individual's welfare as the 'satisfaction of the self-interested preferences that the individual would have after ideal deliberation while thinking clearly with full pertinent information regarding those preferences'.[52] It would, however, be difficult for the following reasons to apply such a measure for the purpose of adjudicating competing claims over worldly resources. Problems would arise on account of the relative opacity of people's level of preference satisfaction to third parties. One would also encounter difficulties of a more theoretical nature in trying

---

[51] He might also want his own conception to be adopted because he believes that its adoption would be most conducive to his own well-being. This, however, might be a mistake, since it might turn out that his well-being as he conceives it is promoted to a greater extent if a conception of welfare other than his own is adopted.

[52] This is the conception that I endorsed in Ch. 1 Sect. III above. (The wording is Richard Arneson's—see Ch. 1, n. 43.)

to arrive at an interpersonal comparison of levels of preference satis-faction even if one assumes the transparency of people's level of pref-erence satisfaction.[53] A more publicly assessable and applicable proxy for preference satisfaction would therefore need to be devised in the light of these difficulties. Such a proxy might, for example, measure an individual's welfare in terms of an intersubjectively constituted list of 'particular goods and conditions that are recognized as important to a good life even by people with divergent values'.[54]

It should be apparent from the above discussion that my endorse-ment of a preference-based conception of welfare or its proxy does not presuppose that I believe that it or its proxy necessarily provides an accurate measure of how well an individual's life is really going in so far as his self-interest is concerned. In fact, I do not believe that wel-fare conceived in either of the above terms would be likely to provide such a measure. Only a conception that measured welfare in terms of the realization of a properly weighted list of all and only those goods that are truly of prudential value would necessarily provide such a measure. It is not hard to see why such a list would probably differ from the preference-based measure, since it is not hard to see how individuals could get things wrong even in the idealized circumstances of clear thinking and full information. Such a list would probably diverge from the aforementioned proxy for the further reason that a list of that which is truly prudentially valuable would probably not track all of the divergent opinions regarding welfare which the proxy must accommodate.

Now I must suppose that either the preference-satisfaction model or its proxy constitutes the right conception of welfare for the pur-poses of distributing worldly resources. Moreover, both of these mod-els will probably be at odds with a variety of more objective conceptions of welfare, including that which is provided by the one true list. Hence, they might seem to fall foul of the stricture of neu-trality that I formulated above. But this is not so. I said that one must *in so far as possible* be neutral amongst various conceptions of welfare.

---

[53] For a discussion of such difficulties see Ronald Dworkin, *Sovereign Virtue* (Cambridge, Mass.: Harvard University Press, 2000), ch. 1.

[54] Here I borrow from T. M. Scanlon, 'The Moral Basis of Interpersonal Comparisons', in Jon Elster and John Roemer (eds.), *Interpersonal Comparisons of Well-Being* (Cambridge: Cambridge University Press, 1991), 17–44, at 39. Scanlon explains (ibid.) that this list is meant to capture a 'shared conception' of 'important ways in which a person's life can be better or worse': 'Some of the ingredients on such a list may be quite specific, such as health, freedom from phys-ical pain, and security against attack. Others may be given by broader categories, such as having opportunities to develop one's capacities, being able to live the kind of life one wants with fam-ily and friends, and having a life that is not in conflict with one's moral and religious beliefs.'

Given the diversity and conflicting nature of the beliefs regarding welfare that people hold, it will, strictly speaking, be impossible to achieve such neutrality completely. Nevertheless, either of the two models sketched above is likely to come closer than more objective accounts of welfare to realizing this neutrality. The preference-satisfaction model attempts to equalize opportunity for welfare where the measure of each individual's welfare is that person's own particular conception of welfare, whatever it might be, as translated into his preferences. Those who affirm the one-true-list conception of welfare might complain that their conception ought to be applied to everyone, and not just to those who happen to believe it. Be that as it may, by adopting the preference-based model people will at least achieve a distribution of resources that measures each individual's welfare by his own lights, even if it does not do that which is impossible when conceptions of the good conflict—which is to measure everyone else's welfare by each individual's own lights. The preference-satisfaction model of welfare more closely approximates a neutrality amongst the particular conceptions of welfare that reasonable people endorse by tailoring each person's share of resources to his particular judgements of what is in his interests.[55] It is also likely that the proxy will approximate such neutrality more closely than would a more objective conception, given that the proxy is constructed precisely with this aim of neutrality in mind.[56]

Finally, I need to acknowledge that even in the presence of a suitably neutral and publicly applicable and assessable conception of welfare for the purposes of interpreting the egalitarian proviso, irreconcilable conflicts arising from competing claims on land cannot be ruled out. It would be difficult to apply the egalitarian proviso to cases in which more than one person or set of persons has a claim on a given plot of land and no substitute plot or other means of compensation would be acceptable to those whose claim is not honoured. Nationalistic identifications of peoples with specific and overlapping stretches of territory are the most obvious source of this difficulty: '[V]ery many of the potential nations of this world live, or until recently have lived, not in compact territorial units but intermixed with each other in complex patterns. It follows that a territorial political unit can only become ethnically homogeneous, in such cases, if it either kills, or expels, or assimilates all non-nationals.'[57] In such circumstances, one can do no

[55] For a further defence of the preference model as an appropriately neutral standard of distributive justice see Arneson, 'Primary Goods Reconsidered', *Noûs*, 24 (1990): 429–54.

[56] See Scanlon, 'The Moral Basis of Interpersonal Comparisons', 39–40.

[57] Ernest Gellner, *Nations and Nationalism* (Oxford: Blackwell, 1983), 2.

better than strive to come as close as possible to the ideal of political voluntarism that I describe in this and the following chapter.[58]

[58] Arend Lijphart's theory of consociational democracy based on a principle of self-determination provides a promising method of approximation. In circumstances in which different groups lay claim to overlapping stretches of territory, he advocates power-sharing by a coalition of parties representing groups whose membership is determined by the voluntary choices of individuals to affiliate with one or another party. Such parties would be represented in the legislative assembly in accordance with a principle of proportional representation. All parties above a certain size would be guaranteed one or more seats in the executive cabinet, and some of them would be granted the power to veto legislation. Lijphart also proposes a 'kind of non-territorial self-determined segmental autonomy' whereby parties can elect to form 'cultural councils' which would, for example, administer 'schools for those who wish to receive an education according to the group's linguistic and cultural traditions' (see Lijphart, 'Self-Determination versus Pre-Determination of Ethnic Minorities in Power-Sharing Systems', in Will Kymlicka (ed.), *The Rights of Minority Cultures* (Oxford: Oxford University Press, 1995), 275–87).

CHAPTER 6

Left-Libertarianism Versus Liberal Egalitarianism

I

Imagine, for the sake of providing an illustration of the ideal of political societies as voluntary associations to which the Lockean left-libertarian aspires, an enormous archipelago that consists of a super-fluity of highly habitable islands of various shapes and sizes. Rapid and inexpensive travel between any two points on this archipelago is possible. It was and remains possible for any group of individuals to stake a claim to an island for the purpose of founding and sustaining a political society while still leaving 'enough and as good' for everyone else—either on her own or in society with others—to improve her situation to the same degree as these founders. An unsettled island is therefore available for anybody who chooses not to join a political society to go off on her own and found a monity. These lone individuals receive full compensation, at little cost to others, for the absence of the benefits of community and hence they are able to thrive to the same degree that others are able to thrive in political society. For those who prefer to live in political society, a sufficiently diverse range of choice of such societies is available so that each has the opportunity to settle in a society which is tailored to her own preferences. Given the diversity and richness of such possibilities, each person has the opportunity to flourish to the same degree as anybody else, either on her own or in society with others. Therefore, any choice to settle in a given political society would constitute free, rational, and informed tacit consent in circumstances of genuine equality. Such circumstances of freedom and equality would serve to liberate the social contract from the confines of the Rawlsian supposition that political society is 'closed' in so far as 'entry into it is only by birth and exit from it is only by death'.[1] It follows from this supposition 'that while social cooperation can be willing and harmonious, and in this sense voluntary, it is not voluntary in the sense that our joining or belonging to associations and groups within society is voluntary'.[2] Political societies in the archipelago, by contrast, would be voluntary associations in both senses of the term. They would not only be willingly embraced but also freely chosen from amongst a sufficiently good range of alternatives.

Some liberal egalitarians are attracted to the principle that the rights-respecting voluntary choices of individuals, including choices to associate with other human beings, should be given full effect when they are made in egalitarian circumstances.[3] The left-libertarian voluntarism that is embodied by the archipelago just described might be regarded as an application of this principle to the choice of one's shared terms of political association with others. Hence, these liberal egalitarians might be tempted to think of the voluntary associations on this archipelago as paragons of legitimately governed political societies.

Before succumbing to such temptation, they should pause to consider the sorts of illiberal or inegalitarian political societies that could, according to the left-libertarian voluntarist, legitimately arise through the free, rational, and informed consent of individuals in this setting. It is an implication of the conception of political voluntarism on offer that a group of people on this archipelago would be entitled to band together and found a society whose outer boundaries mark a threshold the crossing of which constitutes tacit consent to profoundly illiberal or inegalitarian laws. They would be entitled to enact and enforce such laws on the ground that they (or some subset of them) have a rightful claim to this territory, that nobody is forced to enter this territory, and that those who do thereby freely consent in circumstances of equality of opportunity for welfare to submit themselves to the laws of this society. The aim of this chapter is to demonstrate that such illiberal or inegalitarian societies would in fact be legitimate. I acknowledge that this conclusion will run contrary to the instincts of

---

[1] John Rawls, *Political Liberalism* (New York: Columbia University Press, 1993), 40–1. In other words, 'we are not seen as joining society at the age of reason, as we might join an association, but as being born into society where we will lead a complete life' (ibid. 41; see also ibid. 12, 135–6). Cf. Thomas Nagel, *Equality and Partiality* (New York: Oxford University Press, 1991), 36.

[2] Rawls, *Political Liberalism*, 301.

[3] See e.g. Ronald Dworkin, *Sovereign Virtue* (Cambridge, Mass.: Harvard University Press, 2000), introd. and chs. 2–3; G. A. Cohen, 'On the Currency of Egalitarian Justice', *Ethics*, 99 (1989): 906–44; and Richard Arneson, 'Equality and Equal Opportunity for Welfare', *Philosophical Studies*, 56 (1989): 77–93.

certain liberal egalitarians and will try to anticipate and rebut some lines of resistance they might want to offer.

To sharpen the focus of this discussion by providing some illustrations of what is at issue, let us consider the following two sorts of societies that might arise on this archipelago. One of them is characterized by an inegalitarian system of social stratification and the other by the illiberal regulation of the self-regarding behaviour of its members.

One can imagine the following scenario whereby a privately owned plot of land is transformed into an inegalitarian political society. Suppose that, against a fair background of equality of opportunity for welfare, an individual amasses an enormous fortune by dint of effort and risky investments. He stakes a claim to an island. This he may do, since, by hypothesis, his doing so does not disadvantage others. He spends his fortune on the construction of a palace on this island for his own use plus a number of magnificent and luxuriously appointed manor houses for others, each of which is surrounded by elegant private gardens and spacious grounds. He invites others to live on his island, but only on condition that they first enter a lottery which will determine who become the (non-hereditary) lords, ladies, and other noble residents of these manor houses. Each must agree, in exchange for the possibility of becoming a member of this munificently endowed aristocracy for life, to take the risk of being chosen by lot to become a (non-hereditary) serf or servant for life to the lord or lady of one or other of these manors instead.[4] When fully informed of the nature of this gamble, some will find the prospect of becoming a wealthy, privileged aristocrat sufficiently attractive, even when weighed against the prospect of ending up a serf or servant, that it will be rational for them to enter this lottery.[5]

This island is transformed into a political society by the following Lockean process. As a precondition of entering the lottery, each individual is required to enter into an agreement to transfer his rights to legislate and punish to a collective consisting of all of the residents of the island upon completion of the lottery. Each individual is also required to enter into prior agreement to vote, as a member of this

---

[4] For simplicity, I shall assume that the number of people who enter this lottery is the same as the number of people whom the owner is willing to admit on to his island. If the former number exceeds the latter, then a prior lottery will need to be conducted in order to determine who will be allowed to enter the lottery described in the main text.

[5] To render it more plausible that such a gamble would be rational, we might suppose that the odds of becoming a serf or servant rather than an aristocrat are fairly low, since the need to perform menial labour on this island has largely been obviated by automated labour-saving devices. We might also suppose that the luxury of the life of an aristocrat on this island would far surpass the luxury that would be readily available elsewhere.

collective, to entrust the collective's powers of legislation and punishment to the owner of the island and to appoint him sovereign for life on condition that he abide by a Magna Carta which carefully spells out his own duties, powers, and privileges as king as well as the duties and privileges of the nobility and their serfs and servants. By such acts of consent, a legitimate quasi-feudal island kingdom arises on this Lockean archipelago.[6]

To turn to our second example, a highly illiberal city might arise by the following means. A group of individuals stakes a claim to one of the many islands while leaving enough and as good for others. They draw up and unanimously approve an unamendable charter of rules and regulations that places strict puritanical limitations upon sexual practices, manner of dress, the consumption of drugs, freedom of expression, freedom of worship, and the like. They invite others to live on this island, but only on the condition that their setting foot thereupon constitute consent to abide by these rules for however long they remain on the island. Other like-minded individuals flock to this island, and soon we have a shining puritanical city.

The left-libertarian can offer the following more complete explanation of how such an illiberal city could legitimately arise. Assuming that so doing does not disadvantage others, a private individual is entitled to mark the boundaries of her estate as a line which another may cross only if that other thereby tacitly consents, by means of such crossing, to profoundly illiberal rules that govern her household and its grounds. She would, for example, be entitled to admit only those who agree to abide by the aforementioned puritanical limitations. Things would be no different if many individuals each came to acquire legitimate titles of private ownership over contiguous estates that together cover every square inch of, say, an island the size of Manhattan. They could jointly sign a compact that declares that setting foot on any one of their estates constitutes tacit agreement to a set of common illiberal rules. They could mutually agree to transfer the right to enforce these rules within the boundaries of their various estates to a private corporation owned by all and only those who have signed these compacts. To account for the existence of public land which is characteristic of cities, they would also be entitled to donate portions of their estates over to this corporation. This corporately owned land could, by majority vote of the shareholders, be transformed into public streets, parks, plazas, a town hall, and so forth.

---

[6] The society is quasi-feudal rather than strictly feudal because people's social status is not hereditary.

Eventually, by a series of steps, a fully-fledged city will emerge through the transformation of private property rights over contiguous plots of land. Yet at no point, the left-libertarian will claim, will these individuals lose the rights that they had at the outset to govern their plots of land, and whatever they build on this land, in accordance with illiberal principles.

Admittedly, one should be sceptical of any sweeping claim that the rights of governors of political societies to regulate their land are as extensive as the rights of heads of households to do the same. At the very least, one has the following good reason to resist the assimilation of the powers of the governors of a political society to those of the private owners of a household and its grounds. The needs of human beings for freedom of choice of friends and lovers, for privacy, and for personal space provide a sound rationale for a right to illiberal or inegalitarian terms of association in one's house and on its grounds—a right, for example, to exclude people whose political ideology or religious creed one dislikes when choosing whom to invite to dinner or to spend the night. But a right to live in inegalitarian or illiberal political societies is not necessary to meet these needs, and hence the aforementioned rationales for freedom of choice and association in one's own household and its grounds evaporate when the zone of freedom is enlarged so as to encompass an entire political society. For this reason, we cannot simply infer that the rights of the governors of a political society formed by a concatenation of private estates (or the division of a single estate) will mirror the rights of individuals in a state of nature over their privately owned households and their grounds. The legitimate powers of government might turn out to be less than the sum of the legitimate powers of private individuals.

The left-libertarian should acknowledge, in the light of these observations, that one is not necessarily entitled to make the above inference from the rights of private individuals to the rights of governments, since the rationale for the rights of private individuals might not survive their collectivization. Nevertheless, the left-libertarian can point to the following considerations which provide a sound rationale for the claims that people have the right to form highly illiberal or inegalitarian political societies so long as such formation is in accord with the egalitarian proviso and hence neither gives rise to nor preserves inequalities in opportunity for welfare. Each person possesses a right to associate with mutually consenting others on terms of their own choosing. This right of free association is an implication of their several rights of self-ownership. Moreover, when this right is exercised in a manner which accords with the egalitarian proviso, third parties have no complaint which might override this right. They have no complaint because the exercise of this right does not disadvantage anyone in such circumstances.

It should be noted, on behalf of the left-libertarian, that the claim that the aforementioned illiberal and inegalitarian societies are legitimate is nothing more extreme than the claim that those who are governed on such puritanical or quasi-feudal terms have a right to govern themselves in this manner. It follows from this claim that those outside this political society are duty-bound to refrain from coercively interfering with these illiberal or inegalitarian arrangements. But this claim does not also imply any duty on the part of outsiders to provide the members of this society with assistance in enforcing their laws.[7] Nor does this claim imply that the members of the illiberal or inegalitarian political society would be beyond moral censure for governing themselves in this way, since the right to φ is consistent with both the wrongness of φ–ing and blameworthiness for φ-ing.[8]

Puritanically repressive or quasi-feudal societies such as those just imagined could legitimately arise even when we attend to the following limitation on the reach of Lockean consent. One does not offer one's Lockean consent simply by expressly or tacitly registering one's approval or endorsement of the government. Rather, one offers one's Lockean consent by agreeing to transfer some of one's natural rights over person and possessions to the collective that constitutes political society, which thereupon entrusts these powers to the government.[9] A Lockean therefore avoids the following difficulty with the view that the consent of the governed is sufficient to legitimize the authority of government. One can imagine a government that is seriously unjust because it is constitutionally dedicated above all else to sustaining an army consisting of the entire governed population for the purpose of waging wars of pillage against its neighbours. It is a moral fixed point that such a government could not be legitimate, since no such government could genuinely possess the rights to exercise power in this

---

[7] For an explanation of why such a duty would be objectionable see Samuel Freeman, 'Illiberal Libertarians: Why Libertarianism Is Not a Liberal View', *Philosophy and Public Affairs*, 30 (2001): 105–51, at 111–13.

[8] A right to φ consists of a moral immunity from coercive interference in φ-ing rather than an immunity from moral censure for φ-ing. One has, for example, a right to exclude people of a given race from one's dinner party even though one would be worthy of moral censure if one exercised this right. Similarly, the uttering of malicious truths about another may be protected by one's right to freedom of speech, but one would nevertheless be worthy of moral censure for such utterances.

[9] See Ch. 5 n. 3 above. Recall also that, as I noted in Ch. 5 n. 8, for Locke this transfer would be irrevocable in the case of express consent yet revocable in the case of tacit consent.

fashion. Such a government might nevertheless enjoy the free, rational, and informed consent of all of the governed in the following sense: each of the governed could have freely and rationally expressed his well-informed approval of the institutions, constitution, and actions of this government, including its regulation of their lives as soldiers who wage wars of pillage. On a Lockean view, however, such an unjust government could not enjoy the unanimous consent of the governed. This is because consent consists of the transfer of rights that individuals possess in a state of nature rather than the expression of approval of one's government. Since individuals do not have the right to wage wars of pillage in a state of nature, governments could not come to acquire such rights through Lockean consent. The sorts of illiberal or inegalitarian political societies sketched in this section could, by contrast, arise by means of such consensual transfer of rights.

They could legitimately arise even when we attend to the following further constraint that left-libertarian voluntarism imposes. In order to protect the rights of unconsenting members of the next generation, all parents, including those who choose to live in highly illiberal or inegalitarian societies, must fulfil the following three obligations. First, they are obliged to ensure that their children have adequate opportunity to develop the capacity and acquire the knowledge to make free, rational, and informed choices regarding the sort of political society in which they would like to live upon reaching the age of majority. Second, they are obliged to ensure that their children have adequate opportunity to develop the skills, capacities, and knowledge which would enable them to flourish in a range of the political societies on offer. Third, they must not interfere with their children's exercise, upon reaching the age of majority, of their ability to make a free, rational, and informed choice regarding the sort of political society in which they would like to live. It follows that parents may not indoctrinate their children into their preferred way of life or wholly shelter them from outside influences. Rather, they must ensure that their children are provided with schooling which gives them an adequate opportunity to acquire the aforementioned skills, capacities, and knowledge.[10] These obligations might render it unlikely that illiberal

[10] Such a requirement exceeds those of many actually existing liberal societies. The United States Supreme Court, for example, has ruled that Amish parents may exempt their children from schooling beyond the eighth grade. They were exempted from the state's requirement that they ensure that their children are provided with at least two further years of secondary education. The Amish did not object to primary schooling restricted to the teaching of the basic skills of reading, writing, and mathematics. But they objected to secondary schooling on the following grounds: '[The Amish] view secondary school education as an impermissible exposure of their children to a "worldly" influence in conflict with their beliefs. The high school tends to

or inegalitarian political societies would perpetuate themselves via the descendants of the founders. The survival of such societies might instead depend largely on the ability of their founders to recruit new members from the outside. Consequently, many such societies might not be able to sustain themselves beyond the first generation.[11] Nevertheless, the legitimate foundation of such societies is not precluded by the aforementioned obligations to the next generation.

I have shown in this section how one can move from Lockean premisses concerning the natural rights of individuals and their consensual transfer to the conclusion that quasi-feudally inegalitarian or puritanically illiberal political societies could be rendered legitimate by such transfer. In contrast to certain anti-individualistic, communitarian approaches, at no point do I make any fundamental appeal to the rights of groups such as nations, cultures, or societies to govern individuals in illiberal or inegalitarian fashion, where such an appeal is fundamental in so far as group rights are not derived from the rights of individuals. It may be that, on the Lockean approach, a group—a 'body politic', 'society', or 'commonwealth' in Locke's words—with a right to govern in illiberal or inegalitarian fashion can arise by means

---

emphasize intellectual and scientific accomplishments, self-distinction, competitiveness, worldly success, and social life with other students. Amish society emphasizes informal learning-through-doing; a life of "goodness," rather than a life of intellect; wisdom, rather than technical knowledge; community welfare, rather than competition; and separation from, rather than integration with, contemporary worldly society' (US Supreme Court, *Wisconsin* v. *Yoder*, 406 US 205 (1972), at 211). Such an exemption would clearly be at odds with the obligations outlined above.

[11] A further source of difficulty in sustaining such a political society across generations is revealed when we note that, on my interpretation of the egalitarian proviso, the rights of private individuals over land are not bequeathable. Rather, such land must lapse into a state of non-ownership upon the death of an individual (see Ch. 1 Sect. V above). If, for example, an individual's plot of land in a highly illiberal political society must lapse into non-ownership upon his death, does it not become available for a liberal individual to acquire and place under more liberal governance? Not necessarily. For, as A. John Simmons has pointed out to me, so long as this land is located in the interior of the territory of the illiberal political society, and an individual must therefore cross illiberally governed land in order to gain access to it from the world beyond this political society or to the world beyond from it, these others could insist, as a condition of his ever crossing their land, that any individual agree to place this interior plot which he wishes to acquire under the illiberal governance of the political society which surrounds it. (Here I assume that rights of ownership over land carry rights of ownership of the airspace above it.) They would be permitted to impose this restriction so long as the individual is left with enough and as good elsewhere to appropriate and place under more liberal governance. Land at the very edges of an illiberal political society which lapses into non-ownership would be available for individuals to liberate from the jurisdiction of the illiberal society and place under liberal governance, but individuals could be prevented by the method just described from creating liberal enclaves which are entirely surrounded by the illiberal society. (See also Simmons's discussion of 'interior dissenters' in Simmons, 'On the Territorial Rights of States', *Philosophical Issues*, 35 (2001) (supplement to *Noûs*): 300–26, at 314.)

of the consensual transfer of rights from the governed to the collective. But any such group rights are legitimized by, and only by, the free consent of each of the governed. The individual is ultimately sovereign on the Lockean approach, and all other forms of sovereignty must be freely derived from this source.[12]

II

Given his commitments to voluntarism, a Lockean libertarian such as Robert Nozick would not rule out the legitimate rise of highly illiberal or inegalitarian societies. Nozick is not a voluntarist when it comes to the justification of the 'minimal state', since he provides a non-contractualist justification of this state. Yet he believes that such a minimal state provides a 'framework for utopias' within which various communities ranging from the most liberal to the most illiberal would be allowed to form as the result of the free choices of individuals.[13] So long as individuals do not violate the libertarian rights of others—which it is the sole function of this central governing body to enforce—they ought, according to Nozick, to be free to form whatever communities they choose: to exclude whomever they choose from membership in these communities and to include whomever they choose (who also wishes to join this community). Requirements of entry into such a community could include consent to rules that are as illiberal or inegalitarian as the alienability of our rights will allow. Therefore, given Nozick's belief that one has the moral power to sell oneself into permanent slavery or to sell one's organs or one's life, the government of such a community could come, as the result of one's consent, to have absolute power over one's life, limb, or labour.[14] The authority of a dictator who exercises complete control over the lives of

[12] The individualistic, consent-based account of the rise of illiberal or inegalitarian political societies that I have offered is, in certain key respects, similar to the account that Chandran Kukathas has offered in his illuminating 'Are There Any Cultural Rights?' *Political Theory*, 20 (1992): 105–39. I am largely sympathetic to Kukathas's case for the superiority of an individualistic approach to one which makes a fundamental appeal to the rights of groups. The main difference between Kukathas's approach and my own is that he would apparently endorse, and I clearly would not, the claim that illiberal or inegalitarian societies can be legitimate even if they have not arisen in the circumstances of equality illustrated at the outset of this chapter and spelled out more fully in Chs. 1 and 5 above.

[13] See Robert Nozick, *Anarchy, State, and Utopia* (New York: Basic Books, 1974), ch. 10, esp. pp. 309–12.

[14] Nozick writes that 'someone may choose (or permit another) to do to himself *anything* unless he has acquired an obligation to some third party not to do or allow it' (ibid. 58). He affirms the right to sell oneself into slavery at ibid. 331.

the governed who have no right of exit would be justified if they freely and rationally entered into this arrangement. Nozick's libertarianism therefore allows for the formation of puritanical or quasi-feudal communities within his minimal state.[15]

Unlike modern-day libertarians such as Nozick, Locke denies that we have the right to kill ourselves or to sell ourselves into permanent slavery (II. 23). Hence, he denies that we have the right to contract into a political society whose leaders have absolute power over life, limb, or labour. Nevertheless, Locke believes that we have the right to sell ourselves into limited-term indentured servitude (II. 24). He also believes that we have the right to dispose of our possessions as we see fit. Although he acknowledges the alienability of these rights regarding our labour and possessions, he asserts that no rational person would choose to submit to more than a limited regulation of these rights by society:

But though men, when they enter into [political] society, give up the equality, liberty, and executive power they had in the state of nature, into the hands of the society, to be so far disposed of by the legislative, as the good of the society shall require; yet it being only with an intention in every one the better to preserve himself, his liberty and property; (for no rational creature can be supposed to change his condition with an intention to be worse) the power of the society, or *legislative* constituted by them, can *never be supposed to extend farther than the common good*; but is obliged to secure every one's property, by providing against those . . . defects . . . that made the state of nature so unsafe and uneasy. (II. 131)[16]

A government that limits itself to the promotion of the common good does not, according to Locke, have any licence to engage in the paternalistic or otherwise illiberal regulation of the self-regarding behaviour of individuals.[17]

---

[15] Given what he says at ibid. 320–3, Nozick might try to resist this consequence of his views. He might contend that the unanimous consent on which such puritanical or quasi-feudal communities are based would make them unstable and fleeting since they would lose their legitimacy in the face of a single consenter's withdrawal of her consent. But this instability can be eliminated through enforceable contractual agreements to submit to puritanical or quasi-feudal laws as a condition of entering by crossing the boundary of this community. This submission would last for the duration that one remains within the boundaries of this community. (Private clubs are able to maintain the stability of their illiberal or inegalitarian rules by similar means.) Nozick also notes that the ability of members of a community to regulate the behaviour of people on land that is not privately owned (either by a single individual or a group of individuals) is quite limited. I agree, yet I have already shown how a community could arise on land all of which is privately owned by members of that community.

[16] See also ch. 11 of the *Second Treatise* (esp. II. 135) and II. 171 and II. 222.

[17] See Locke, *A Letter concerning Toleration* (Indianapolis, Ind.: Hackett, 1983).

Contrary to Locke, I do not think one can plausibly argue that it would be irrational for an individual to consent to the illiberal or inegalitarian societies sketched in Section I above. It is not, for example, necessarily irrational for an individual freely to choose to enter into the contemplative life of a monastic order with exacting vows of chastity, poverty, and obedience.[18] Nor is it necessarily irrational for one freely to choose to enter into the highly regimented life of the military. Nor is it necessarily irrational to gamble with one's freedom for the prospect of great gain. One who makes such choices need not be of such unsound mind that he would be deemed incapable of entering into legally binding contractual agreements that give rise to weighty obligations. Nor need a person make such choices with an intention to worsen his condition.[19]

In his *Letter concerning Toleration* Locke argues that it is legitimate for a 'free and voluntary Society' such as a church to impose rules and regulations upon its members that promote the proper public worship of God and 'by means thereof the acquisition of Eternal Life'.[20] He argues that 'since the joining together of several members into this church-society . . . is absolutely free and spontaneous, it necessarily follows, that the right of making its laws can belong to none but the society itself'.[21] In such a society 'no man will have a legislator imposed upon him, but whom himself has chosen'.[22] Presumably a church is entitled to impose, as a condition of membership, requirements concerning an individual's religious beliefs, speech, and personal conduct. Some such requirements might differ on the basis of one's gender, as might the privileges extended to the members of this church. Many of these rules would be regarded as highly illiberal or inegalitarian if imposed as a condition of inclusion into a political society. Locke does not, in his *Letter*, describe a 'Commonwealth' (i.e.

[18] It might, of course, be irrational to hold many of the superstitious religious beliefs that are held by some members of actually existing monastic orders. So let us imagine a life of meditation, contemplation, and discipline that is purged of such superstition.

[19] According to Simmons: 'Considerations of the quality of government (what it would be rational to consent to) also serve to help specify the content of political consent in Locke. Political consent is often tacit, according to Locke, and it is initially unclear just what tacit consent is consent *to*' (Simmons, *On the Edge of Anarchy* (Princeton, NJ: Princeton University Press, 1993), 209). He proposes that the content of one's tacit consent is supplied by that which it would be rational to consent to, which is, according to both Locke and Simmons, nothing that exceeds a liberal government whose powers are limited to the promotion of the common good. I have already questioned the claim that it would not be rational to consent to an illiberal or inegalitarian government. Here I would like to point out that an illiberal or inegalitarian government would be free to resolve any ambiguity or unclarity by publicly declaring that tacit consent is consent precisely to the illiberal or inegalitarian terms of the charter that governs this society.

[20] Locke, *A Letter concerning Toleration*, 30.   [21] Ibid. 28–9.   [22] Ibid. 29.

political society) as a 'free and voluntary Society'. Yet two of the essential qualities that he attributes to a voluntary society are, according to him, shared by a political society. They are (1) that 'No body is born a member' or 'by nature is bound unto' such a society, but (2) rather that 'every one joins himself voluntarily'.[23] For Locke, the main feature that distinguishes a political society from a voluntary society (such as a church) is the different ends or purposes for which individuals form or join these societies.[24] In the case of a political society, they join only to protect their life, liberty, and possessions against invasions, while in the case of the church they join for the salvation of their soul. If, however, I am correct in arguing that it is not necessarily irrational for individuals freely to consent to the authority of a government that imposes illiberal or inegalitarian constraints that go beyond the protection of life, liberty, and possessions against invasions, then I cannot see how Locke could deny the legitimacy of such an illiberal or inegalitarian government, given his voluntarist commitments, and particularly in the light of his claims regarding the authority of the church.[25]

III

Contrary to the left-libertarian position that I have advanced, some would insist that liberal-egalitarian principles are mandatory throughout the land even in the face of the free, rational, and informed Lockean consent, in circumstances of equality, of some of the governed to contrary illiberal or inegalitarian principles. They would insist that the inegalitarian and illiberal societies described in Section I above clearly overstep uncontroversial and unbreachable limits to the reach of legitimate political authority. Hence, they would regard the left-libertarian's conclusion that such societies are legitimate as either a *reductio ad absurdum* of one or more of the premises of this account of political legitimacy or the product of invalid inference.

[23] Ibid. 28. A third quality that Locke identifies, freedom of exit, is not, according to him, shared by those who are members in a political society by express consent. Yet it is not clear that Locke is justified in asserting such a disanalogy between a political and a voluntary society.

[24] See ibid.

[25] I should note that Simmons is in agreement that Lockean consent might legitimate highly illiberal societies: '[S]ocieties whose structures have been legitimated (in the Lockean sense) by the free, unanimous consent of their members may have quite illiberal shapes without thereby losing their legitimacy. Highly restrictive religious orders or extremely conservative agricultural communes, empowered by the free, informed consent of all members, could count as perfectly legitimate "societies" on the Lockean model' (Simmons, 'Justification and Legitimacy', *Ethics*, 109 (1999): 739–71, at 761 n. 51).

A defender of mandatory liberal egalitarianism throughout the land might argue that the aforementioned puritanical and quasi-feudal societies are illegitimate because they fall foul of a duty on the part of those in authority to treat those whom they govern as free and equal.[26] Such a liberal egalitarian might advance the claim that the duty of those in authority to treat the governed as *free* implies a duty not to subject them to laws which would deprive them of familiar basic liberties. Because the governors of both types of society fail to safeguard basic liberal freedoms, they would violate such a duty even though all of the governed have consented to live in a society in which such liberties are unprotected.[27] Moreover, a constitutionally hierarchical, class-divided, quasi-feudal society would be ruled out on the further ground that it would violate a duty on the part of those in authority to treat those whom they govern as *equals*.

In answering this critic, the left-libertarian could acknowledge the existence of a duty on the part of governors to treat those whom they govern as free and equal. Yet he would want to resist the interpretation of this duty which this liberal egalitarian offers. The left-libertarian would maintain that this duty is fully discharged through respect for the free, rational, and informed choices of individuals which are made in circumstances of equality. In particular, the left-libertarian would maintain that a duty to treat the governed as free implies nothing more or less than a duty to uphold the rights of mutually consenting individuals to freedom of political association on whatever terms they choose, including highly illiberal ones, so long as these choices are not disruptive of equality. Indeed, the left-libertarian would maintain that the liberal egalitarian fails to treat the governed as free because he places restrictions upon their choice of terms of political association in a manner which is inconsistent with full respect for their status as autonomous, rational choosers.[28] The left-libertarian would maintain

[26] If this argument is sound, then the Rawlsian assumption that political societies are involuntary associations turns out to be inessential to the case for liberal egalitarianism, since quasi-feudal, puritanically repressive, or otherwise highly illiberal or inegalitarian political societies would be illegitimate even among the voluntary associations of the archipelago.

[27] Rawls, for example, maintains that 'the basic liberties are inalienable', by which he means that 'any agreement by citizens which waives or violates a basic liberty, however rational and voluntary this agreement may be, is void *ab initio*; that is, it has no legal force and does not affect any citizen's basic liberties' (Rawls, *Political Liberalism*, 365). (Rawls's claim of inalienability might, however, rest upon the presupposition that political society is closed rather than a voluntary association (see ibid. 366–7). See also my discussion of Rawls in the next section.) I should note that Ronald Dworkin, whom I have also described as a liberal egalitarian, has not, as far as I am aware, explicitly pronounced in his published work on the question of whether the basic liberties are inalienable.

[28] For some remarks which are relevant to a defence of the claim that the right to alienate one's basic liberties is more in keeping with one's moral status as an autonomous agent than the denial

that the duty to treat the governed as equals implies nothing more or less than a duty to ensure that the choices of individuals regarding political association are made against background conditions of, and which are preservative of, equality of opportunity for welfare. When such egalitarian conditions are met, even quasi-feudal political societies are legitimate.

IV

John Rawls has argued that liberal egalitarianism should prevail throughout the land by virtue of the hypothetical consent of all of the governed to such liberal policies. More precisely, liberal egalitarianism should prevail throughout all parts of a typically large and pluralistic modern state because some who live within its borders could reasonably reject illiberal or inegalitarian principles, yet none could reasonably reject liberal-egalitarian principles.[29] In this concluding section I will argue for the superiority of a Lockean left-libertarian voluntarism grounded in actual consent over a Rawlsian liberal egalitarianism grounded in such hypothetical consent among those who have not chosen their political society.

Defenders of the Rawlsian stance are insufficiently attuned to the possibility that like-minded members of a local subpopulation within a large and pluralistic state might come to a unanimous, free, rational, and informed decision to govern themselves in accordance with illiberal or inegalitarian principles. The left-libertarian voluntarist can grant that those in the larger state but outside such local units could reasonably reject such illiberal or inegalitarian principles if these principles were applied throughout the land. But given that these outsiders would neither be governed nor disadvantaged by these locally applied principles, it is difficult to see how any reason these outsiders would

of such a right see my 'Kamm on the Morality of Killing', *Ethics*, 108 (1997): 197–207, at 205–7. For a rebuttal of the Kantian argument that 'some rights we cannot surrender without becoming less than fully human or degrading human dignity; these rights are as a result inalienable' see Simmons, *On the Edge of Anarchy*, 140, 142–3.

[29] See Rawls, *Political Liberalism*. Rawls writes that 'our exercise of political power is fully proper only when it is exercised in accordance with a constitution the essentials of which all citizens as free and equal may reasonably be expected to endorse in the light of principles and ideals acceptable to their common human reason. This is the liberal principle of legitimacy' (ibid. 137; cf. 217). Rawls relates the principle of legitimacy to the hypothetical contractual device of the original position by proposing that we 'look at the question of legitimacy from the point of view of the original position' and 'try to show that the principles of justice they [the parties in the original position] would adopt would in effect incorporate this principle of legitimacy' (ibid. 137 n. 5).

have to reject such principles would bear on the rights of these insiders to govern themselves locally in accord with these principles. Why should those outside and unaffected by this local unit have any standing to override the free, rational, informed, and unanimous choice of those within the local unit to govern themselves in accord with such principles?

The Rawlsian hypothetical-consent theorist simply takes the borders of the political society in which the hypothetical consenters reside for granted. But, as the previous paragraph makes clear, the principles of governance that one could reasonably endorse or reject will vary in accordance with the size and composition of the political society in question. The hypothetical-contract theorist must therefore provide a non-arbitrary means of drawing the boundaries of the society in question. By contrast, the Lockean approach leaves the borders of political societies to be fixed by the actual consent of individuals.

As I noted in Section I above, Rawls's liberal egalitarianism rests upon the assumption that political society is an involuntary form of association in the following respect: it is a closed society that is entered only by birth and exited from only by death. He maintains that liberal-egalitarian principles must prevail throughout the land in such closed societies. Nothing that I have said in this book amounts to a refutation of this last claim. Perhaps a liberal egalitarian such as Rawls could grant, if only for the sake of argument, that liberal-egalitarian principles need not prevail throughout the land in the ideal circumstances of the open confederation of societies on the archipelago that were sketched above. Rather, the illiberal and inegalitarian societies described above would, in fact, be legitimized by the actual consent of the governed in these imagined circumstances. The liberal egalitarian might, however, advance the factual premiss that the openness of the societies on the archipelago could not be realized in practice. We must instead reconcile ourselves to the relatively closed societies of the sort in which we actually live—societies which have not been and cannot be legitimized by means of actual tacit consent that is freely offered in circumstances of genuine equality.[30]

---

[30] Cf. Rawls: 'I believe that a democratic society is not and cannot be a community, where by a community I mean a body of persons united in affirming the same comprehensive . . . doctrine. The fact of reasonable pluralism which characterizes a society with free institutions makes this impossible. This is the fact of profound and irreconcilable differences in citizens' reasonable comprehensive religious and philosophical conceptions of the world, and in their view of the moral and aesthetic values to be sought in human life . . .

Again, political society is not, and cannot be, an association. We do not enter it voluntarily. Rather we simply find ourselves in a particular political society at a certain moment of historical time. We might think our presence in it, our being here, is not free' (Rawls, *Justice as Fairness: A Restatement* (Cambridge, Mass.: Harvard University Press, 2001), 3–4).

I reject the factual premiss. There is no practical barrier to the transformation of a political society such as the United States into something much more like a confederation of voluntary associations in which individuals are allowed to migrate into uninhabited areas and establish the illiberal or inegalitarian societies imagined above. Even in more densely populated territories individuals could be allowed to migrate in a manner that gives rise to the gradual transformation of villages or neighbourhoods, and eventually entire cities or regions, into enclaves of illiberalism or inegalitarianism.

Rawls argues that the right of emigration would not be sufficient to legitimate illiberal or inegalitarian political societies:

[N]ormally leaving one's country is a grave step: it involves leaving the society and culture in which we have been raised, the society and culture whose language we use in speech and thought to express and understand ourselves, our aims, goals, and values; the society and culture whose history, customs, and conventions we depend on to find our place in the social world . . .

The government's authority cannot, then, be freely accepted in the sense that the bonds of society and culture, of history and social place of origin, begin so early to shape our life and are normally so strong that the right of emigration . . . does not suffice to make accepting its authority free, politically speaking, in the way that liberty of conscience suffices to make accepting ecclesiastical authority free, politically speaking.[31]

. . . While the principles [of justice] adopted [by the hypothetical contractors] will no doubt allow for emigration . . . they will not permit arrangements that would be just only if emigration were allowed. The attachments formed to persons and places, to associations and communities, as well as cultural ties, are normally too strong to be given up . . . Thus the right to emigrate does not affect what counts as a just basic structure, for this structure is to be viewed as a scheme into which people are born and are expected to lead a complete life.[32]

It should be noted that Rawls's argument does not presuppose that individuals would have any difficulty in gaining permission to settle, or in securing gainful employment, in another political society. He refers only to the costs and difficulties of severing ties with the political society of one's birth rather than to any of the further costs or difficulties of establishing a place in another political society.

This argument is compelling in the context of the large scale of many actually existing political societies. In this context, the severing of ties with one's political society often implies the travelling of some great distance, both geographically and culturally. It is plausible to

---

[31] Rawls, *Political Liberalism*, 222.   [32] Ibid. 277.

suppose that it would be impossible fully to compensate an individual for the cost of severing such ties. But Rawls's argument loses its force in the context of the left-libertarian voluntarism under consideration. When one is surrounded by a loose confederation of political societies of various shapes, sizes, and ideological orientations within a single nation, rather than a relatively large and politically monolithic unit which roughly corresponds to the boundaries of a nation, the cost of leaving the illiberal or inegalitarian political society of one's birth will tend to be much lower. It might involve nothing more extreme than the cost of moving to another town or region of an actually existing nation-state. Surely it is an exaggeration to maintain that such costs would be so great as to render the right to emigrate—i.e. the right to migrate from one political society to another within the confederation in question—irrelevant to the justification of the authority of the political society in which one lives. So long as there is sufficient opportunity for those who are born in illiberal or inegalitarian political societies to migrate upon reaching the age of majority to liberal-egalitarian political societies that are not so geographically or culturally removed, the right to migrate would serve to legitimate these illiberal and inegalitarian societies. Hence, the Rawlsian argument does not stand in the way of the transformation of a liberal-egalitarian nation-state into a left-libertarian national confederation in which like-minded individuals are permitted to found profoundly illiberal or inegalitarian towns, cities, or provinces so long as the confederation also contains liberal-egalitarian political societies to which individuals may migrate without difficulty.

The Lockean project should be seen as an attempt to realize those conditions of freedom, equality, and rational and informed choice which would ensure that residence in a given political society constitutes morally binding actual tacit consent to the authority of the government of that society. Rather than imposing, as the Rawlsian liberal egalitarian would, that form of government to which individuals should but do not all actually agree, the Lockean leaves it to actually consenting individuals, in concert with other actually consenting individuals, to make their own choices regarding the nature of their government. And, rather than taking the boundaries of the political society in which individuals live as given and entered only by birth and exited from only by death, for the Lockean the boundaries of political societies are once again the product of the actual choices of individuals. Rawls claims:

No society can, of course, be a scheme of cooperation which men enter voluntarily in a literal sense; each person finds himself placed at birth in some particular position in some particular society, and the nature of this position materially affects his life prospects. Yet a society satisfying the principles of justice as fairness comes as close as a society can to being a voluntarily scheme, for it meets the principles which free and equal persons would assent to under circumstances that are fair. In this sense its members are autonomous and the obligations they recognize self-imposed.[33]

On the basis of what has been said in this and the previous chapter, we can now see how a left-libertarian voluntarist society comes closer than the Rawlsian society to the ideal of political society as a voluntary association.[34] In this sense its members are more autonomous than Rawlsian citizens and the obligations they recognize more genuinely self-imposed.

[33] Rawls, *A Theory of Justice* (Cambridge, Mass.: Harvard University Press, 1971), 13. (Cf. Nagel, *Equality and Partiality*, 8, 36.)

[34] I share Simmons's suspicion that there is something half-hearted in Rawls's claim that he is guided by the ideal of political society as a voluntary association. Simmons infers such lack of commitment from Rawls's lack of interest in various measures that would make membership in political society more voluntary, 'such as offering various classes of citizenship (and "resident noncitizen") options, training and support to make emigration and resettlement a more realistic option, programs to disseminate relevant information, a more formalized choice procedure, and so on' (Simmons, 'Justification and Legitimacy', 761). Moreover, given that Lockean voluntarism is, as we have seen, capable of justifying highly illiberal societies, I concur with Simmons that Rawls's 'gesture toward voluntarism just seems inconsistent with the [liberal] spirit of his project' (ibid. n. 51). (See Ch. 6 n. 25 above, which contains a quotation from the footnote in which Simmons points to this inconsistency.)

CHAPTER 7

The Problem of
Intergenerational Sovereignty

The past is a foreign country . . .
(L. P. Hartley, *The Go-Between*)

Imagine that in the not-too-distant future the members of a highly representative and democratically reformed British Parliament draft an ideal Bill of Rights.[1] Unlike any before it, this one protects all and only those rights that ought to be protected. It is far superior to the American Bill of Rights which was drafted over two centuries ago. Suppose that the British declare by Act of Parliament that this bill applies not just to Great Britain, but also to the United States of America. They declare that it constitutes an amendment to the Constitution of the United States which supersedes the old American Bill of Rights plus any other provisions of the US Constitution that are not in accord with the new bill. In a generous spirit they add that Americans shall have the power to repeal this amendment by the very same procedure for amending their Constitution that is set forth in Article V of that document: a two-thirds majority of each of the two houses of Congress plus a simple majority of three-quarters of the state legislatures.

To the objection that this amendment, no matter how perfect in substance, is illegitimate because it lacks the democratic consent of the governed, the British offer the following reply: 'Your own Bill of Rights is no more democratic in its origins than our new one. No living American ever cast a vote in favour of the old Bill of Rights or in favour of those officials who drafted and ratified it. To make matters

---

[1] We shall assume that Britain in this thought-experiment is now a republic rather than a constitutional monarchy.

worse from the standpoint of democracy, your old Bill of Rights was drafted and ratified by profoundly undemocratic assemblies that consisted of élites of white male property-owners to the exclusion of all others. These men made their work no easier to amend than the new Bill of Rights. The old Bill of Rights was a dead hand from the past, emanating from an undemocratic body of men who have long since perished. It placed severe limits on what democratically elected majorities could do in the present. Why should you be any less outraged by the profoundly undemocratic origins of the old Bill of Rights than the new?'

The complaint that the American Constitution (including its Bill of Rights) is a dead hand from the past is a familiar one among some present-day democratic theorists. Their complaint is directed against the entrenchment of these laws against repeal by anything less than a *super-majority* of the (democratically elected representatives of the) living, where this super-majority greatly exceeds fifty per cent plus one.[2] The dead are able from their graves to thwart the will of a simple majority of the living, which seems an offence to democracy. Although these democrats are opposed to a Constitution that can be amended only by a super-majority, they do not object to constitutions and statutes handed down from the dead which can be repealed by a simple majority vote of the living, as is roughly speaking the case in Britain.[3] So long as the living have the power to repeal the laws of the dead by simple majority vote, these democrats have no objection to their being ruled by these laws in the absence of any simple majority vote of the living to repeal.[4]

In this chapter I would like to consider an argument against the legitimacy of constitutions such as the American Constitution, and against laws more generally that were enacted by those who are now dead, that is far more radical than the argument of the democrat theorists to which I have just referred. This argument is contained in a famous letter by Thomas Jefferson which he sent to James Madison in

---

[2] It is accompanied by a condemnation of the institution of Supreme Court judicial review, in which 'unelected judges' exercise the power to strike down acts of present-day legislators which they deem to be in conflict with the Constitution.

[3] I say 'roughly speaking' because it is indirectly through their elected representatives in Parliament that the people have this power, and not directly. Whenever I speak in this chapter of laws being enacted or repealed by 'a majority vote of the living', this should be read to mean 'a majority vote of adult citizens (in the case of direct democracy) or of their democratically elected representatives'. I adopt this shorthand for the sake of ease of expression.

[4] I believe that Robert Dahl would subscribe to all of the views that I have just attributed to 'some present-day democratic theorists' (see Dahl, *Democracy and its Critics* (New Haven, Conn.: Yale University Press, 1989)).

the year in which Congress proposed the Bill of Rights.[5] In this letter Jefferson argues that, since '*the earth belongs . . . to the living*' and not the dead, laws passed by those who are now dead should have no authority over the living.[6] He concludes that every law, including those that make up the Constitution itself, should lapse nineteen years after its enactment unless it is re-enacted for another nineteen years by a majority vote of those living at the time of its re-enactment. Any law that is not so re-enacted would automatically be struck from the books. Jefferson proposes the figure of nineteen years on the basis of an analysis of 'the tables of mortality' available to him. He calculated that, on average, once that number of years had elapsed we would reach the point at which a majority of those who were alive and of voting age when this law was passed would have died. Jefferson regards this point in time as morally significant for the following reason.[7] He supposes that the citizens of voting age in a given political society at a given point in time constitute the members of a single generation.[8] He also recognizes that in any large political society we can be fairly certain that on any given day some people will reach the age of majority and others will die. Hence, the set of people who constitute the generation of citizens of voting age in a given political society on a given day will not be identical to the set of people who constitute this generation on the next day, assuming that the generation persists from one day to the next. Barring dramatic events, there will not be much change in the composition of such a generation from day to day. But over time these small changes will accumulate to such a degree that the generation which existed at that significantly earlier point in time will no longer exist. Jefferson believes that the point of non-existence would be reached when a majority of those alive at that earlier point in time had died. Suppose now that a law was enacted at time t_0 by the generation of those who were eligible to vote at that time. Suppose that t_1 is that point in time at which a majority of those alive at t_0 have died. If this

---

[5] Thomas Jefferson, Letter to James Madison, 6 Sept. 1789, in *Thomas Jefferson: Writings*, ed. Merrill D. Peterson (New York: Library of America, 1984), 959–64.

[6] Ibid. 959.

[7] The line of reasoning which I am about to sketch involves some reconstruction and filling in of the details of that which is, I think, fairly clearly implicit in Jefferson's letter even if not always explicitly spelled out.

[8] Jefferson, Letter to Madison, 961. Here Jefferson departs somewhat from the common usage of the term 'generation', since he supposes that every voting member of a political society alive at a given point in time would be a member of the same generation no matter how many years separate the youngest from the oldest and no matter whether this single generation includes the children or even grandchildren of some of its members. Cf.: '**generation** *n.* 1 all of the people born and living at about the same time, regarded collectively' (Judy Pearsall (ed.), *Concise Oxford Dictionary*, 10th edn. (Oxford: Oxford University Press, 2001), 590).

law continues to bind the living beyond t_1, then the dead hand of the past would impose itself on the living, since the living would be under the authority of a law enacted by a generation which has since passed from the scene. Indeed, Jefferson goes so far as to proclaim that a law that is enforced for longer than nineteen years 'is an act of force and not of right'.[9] His resistance to the rule of the dead over the living is more thoroughgoing than that of the democratic theorists to which I referred a moment ago, since he objects to the legitimacy of even those laws passed down from the dead that could be repealed by a simple majority of the living.

In resisting the view that laws would retain their legitimacy if they could be repealed by a simple majority of the living, Jefferson points to practical impediments in an imperfect democracy to the repeal of a law by even a simple majority. He says:

It may be said that the succeeding generation exercising in fact the power of repeal, this leaves them as free as if the constitution or law had been expressly limited to 19 years only . . . [This might hold] if every form of government were so perfectly contrived that the will of the majority could always be obtained fairly and without impediment. But this is true of no form. The people cannot assemble themselves; their representation is unequal and vicious. Various checks are opposed to every legislative proposition. Factions get possession of the public councils. Bribery corrupts them. Personal interests lead them astray from the general interests of their constituents; and other impediments arise so as to prove to every practical man that a law of limited duration is much more manageable than one which needs a repeal.[10]

In his letter to Madison, Jefferson also offers the rudiments of a more principled, less pragmatic, and hence more philosophically satisfying reply to the claim that the power of the living to repeal the laws of the dead by majority vote is sufficient to render the authority of these laws over the living unproblematic. For he maintains that 'We seem not to have perceived that, by the law of nature, one generation is to another as one independant nation to another'.[11] Assuming the truth of this claim, Jefferson could have offered the following reply to the claim that the power to repeal them by simple majority vote is enough to legitimize the laws of the dead. He could have noted that if a foreign country were to declare that its laws apply to the United

---

[9] Jefferson, Letter to Madison, 963.　　　　[10] Ibid. 963.

[11] Ibid. 962. This analogy recurs in Jefferson's writing. Nearly twenty-five years later, for example, he writes: 'We may consider each generation as a distinct nation, with a right, by the will of its majority, to bind themselves, but none to bind the succeeding generation, more than the inhabitants of another country' (Jefferson, Letter to John Wayles Eppes, 24 June 1813, in *Thomas Jefferson: Writings*, 1280).

States, that country would hardly silence the complaint that these laws lacked any authority over Americans by pointing out that their declaration also grants Americans the power to repeal these laws by a simple majority. Britain, in the example with which I began this chapter, would not silence defenders of democracy by modifying their decree so that it grants Americans the power to repeal their new Bill of Rights by a simple majority vote. Americans would not need to muster a majority vote in order to get themselves out from under the authority of these foreign laws. A majority vote would be unnecessary even if all of the practical impediments to doing so that Jefferson lists in the passage quoted above were absent. Rather, these British laws would simply fail to bind Americans.

In the light of the absence of authority of the present-day British to impose their laws on Americans, how can one defend the claim that laws enacted by a deceased generation of Americans have any authority over the present generation? More generally, how can one defend the claim that laws enacted by a deceased generation of citizens of country x have any authority over the present generation of citizens of country x? The problem of intergenerational sovereignty which figures in the title of this chapter is that of providing a satisfactory answer to these questions. As I hope to have made clear already, this problem is not unique to those countries such as the United States with written constitutions that are entrenched against repeal by simple majority vote and in which the judiciary is vested with the power to strike down recently enacted statutes that come into conflict with these entrenched provisions. It also applies to a country such as Britain where, roughly speaking, any law may be repealed by a simple majority vote of the present-day House of Commons and the judiciary cannot strike down any Acts of Parliament.

I shall argue in this chapter that as things now stand the laws of the dead do not legitimately bind the living in present-day societies. My defence of this claim will consist of the rejection of three attempts to justify the authority of the dead over the living at present—the first consequentialist; the second collectivist; and the third based on a theory of tacit consent which James Madison proposes in his reply to Jefferson's letter.

Given the present-day illegitimacy of the laws of the dead over the living, I believe that a Jeffersonian practice of periodic renewal of the laws would be a significant improvement over the way things are. But I shall show in the concluding section of this chapter that such a Jeffersonian practice would not itself justify the authority of the laws of the dead over all of the living. It would fail to generate an obligation to obey these laws in the case of many young adults who are beyond the age of majority. I shall explain how this shortcoming of Jefferson's proposal can be overcome by the realization of a Lockean ideal of free and equal tacit consent which differs from the aforementioned Madisonian theory of tacit consent. Moreover, such Lockean consent would justify the authority of the laws of the dead over the young in a manner which would render Jefferson's proposal superfluous. These observations will provide additional support for the claim that Lockean consent is both a necessary and a sufficient condition of legitimate political authority. One lesson to be drawn from this chapter is that the authority over the living of laws passed by those who are now dead is especially difficult to justify in the absence of the Lockean consent of the living.

Before turning to these tasks, I would like to offer the following minor amendment and illustration of Jefferson's proposal.

We should take account of the fact that the demographic information on which Jefferson drew is now out of date. The life expectancy of an adult is now much longer than it was in his day.[12] If we were to calculate the number of years which would need to elapse before a majority of those adults alive at a given point in time will have died, the figure would turn out to be significantly greater than nineteen years. Nevertheless, it would not be wise to revise Jefferson's figure simply in the light of this fact, since we will also want to accommodate certain variables which Jefferson ignores. For simplicity, Jefferson assumes a birth rate equal to the death rate and also assumes the absence of any other factors which might give rise to population growth. Given these assumptions, the first point t_1 $(t_1 > t_0)$ at which a majority of those adults members of a political society alive at t_0 will have died will be identical to the first point t_* $(t_* > t_0)$ at which a majority of those adult members of the political society alive at t_* will not have been adult members of this political society at t_0. But the population might grow on account of a birth rate in excess of the death rate, immigration in excess of emigration, or an expansion of the boundaries of the political society. In the case of a growing population, the first point t_* will come sooner than the first point t_1. Perhaps we

---

[12] Jefferson's calculations were based in part on the estimate that someone who had just reached the age of majority of 21 had a life expectancy of 34 more years (Letter to Madison, 960–1). By contrast, an American who turned 21 in 1999 had a life expectancy of 56.8 more years. It is also relevant that the age of majority in the United States is now 18 rather than 21. Someone who turned 18 in 1999 had a life expectancy of 59.6 more years (see Robert Anderson and Peter DeTurk, 'United States Life Tables, 1999', *National Vital Statistics Report*, 50/6 (Hyattsville, Md.: National Center for Health Statistics, 21 March 2002), 7).

should say that the generation of adult members of a given political society at t_0 passes from the scene at this sooner point $t*$ when the two points diverge. Given the much longer life expectancy of our day, even this sooner point $t*$ is likely to arrive later than nineteen years from t_0. But to err on the side of caution—as we ought to in order to make sure that the living do not end up being ruled by the dead hand of a generation which has in fact passed from the scene—we should exercise restraint in revising Jefferson's figure of nineteen years upward. In the discussion which follows I shall update Jefferson's figure by slightly amending it to the round figure of twenty years.

As Jefferson makes clear, the logic of his argument applies not just to statutes enacted by the legislature, but with equal force to those laws which form the very constitution which legitimizes the institutions of government including the legislature itself. Whatever procedure is deemed appropriate for the enactment of a constitution ought to apply to its re-enactment as well. For believers in popular sovereignty, a referendum of the people is the most appropriate means of enacting a constitution. Hence, it should periodically be re-enacted by popular referendum rather than by an act of the legislature.[13] We might suppose, for the purposes of illustration, that the procedure of re-enactment of the Constitution and other laws of society is institutionalized in the following form. Every twentieth year that Americans go to the polls to elect a president and Members of Congress they would first express a preference for or against the re-enactment of the Constitution. Assuming that the Constitution is re-enacted by such referendum and a president and Congress duly elected, the newly convened Congress would take a vote for or against the re-enactment of all statutes on the books for another twenty years. Procedures would be established to exclude certain controversial laws from this vote on

---

[13] Véronique Munoz-Dardé raises the following interesting question: Presumably one of the clauses of this Constitution will declare that laws and the Constitution must be re-enacted every so many years. Is *this* clause also subject to periodic re-enactment? Or is it, perhaps uniquely, exempt from the requirement of re-enactment? If it is exempt, on what grounds? If it is not exempt, then what will happen if the people fail to re-enact it? Will the requirement for re-enactment of the laws and the Constitution thereby cease? My response is that everything, including this very clause, is subject to re-enactment. This clause ought perpetually to be re-enacted. But if it is not re-enacted, it does not follow that the laws need no longer be re-enacted. If this clause is allowed to lapse, and laws are no longer re-enacted, what follows is (1) that the laws lose their moral legitimacy once they pass the date by which they ought to have expired and (2) that, regrettably, this moral fact is no longer legally recognized. This case is no different from a case in which, say, a constitutional provision calling for universal franchise is allowed to lapse or is repealed and is replaced by one which restricts the franchise to members of the majority race.

re-enactment *en masse*, so they could be debated and voted upon separately.[14]

I shall now turn to a consideration of the first of three attempts to justify the authority of the dead over the living.

1. *A consequentialist argument.* One might acknowledge that Jefferson's proposal is very nice in theory but insist that it would never work in practice. Consider Madison's own response to Jefferson's letter addressed to him:

However applicable in theory the doctrine [of renewal after nineteen years] may be to a Constitution, it seems liable in practice to some weighty objections.

Would not a Government ceasing of necessity at the end of a given term, unless prolonged by some Constitutional Act, previous to its expiration, be too subject to the casualty and consequences of an interregnum?

Would not a Government so often revised become too mutable and novel to retain that share of prejudice in its favor which is a salutary aid to the most rational Government?

Would not such periodical revision engender pernicious factions that might not otherwise come into existence; and agitate the public mind more frequently and more violently than might be expedient?[15]

Might one justifiably conclude that the laws of the dead must be assumed to have authority by default over the living in the light of the disastrous consequences of the lapse of such authority? This conclusion would be too hasty, since this consequentialist objection to the periodic renewal of the Constitution and other laws is not necessarily an argument in favour of automatically being bound by dead Americans; rather it is an argument in favour of automatically being bound by a set of laws that will ensure civilized order rather than anarchy. These laws could just as well be supplied by a foreign country such as Britain.

Even if, as is no doubt the case, one could produce a consequentialist argument that it is better to be bound by past generations of one's own country rather than by the laws of a foreign country, Madison's argument will still fail unless it can be shown that anarchy would

---

[14] A similar procedure of re-enactment in a British republic governed by a democratically reformed Parliament might be institutionalized as follows: A popular referendum on its Constitution would be scheduled to coincide with the general election of a government roughly every twenty years. Assuming that this referendum passes and a government is elected, Parliament would convene in order to vote on the re-enactment of statutes shortly after this election.

[15] James Madison, Letter to Thomas Jefferson, 4 February 1790, in *The Writings of James Madison*, ed. Gaillard Hunt, 9 vols. (New York: G. P. Putnam's Sons, 1904), v. 438 n.–439 n.

prevail if the laws passed by previous generations of Americans were allowed to lapse without periodic re-enactment. In the light of the threat of anarchy, it is likely that citizens and their elected representatives would act on the presumption that the Constitution and other laws warrant re-enactment unless a very strong case for their abandonment can be made. Those elected representatives in legislatures throughout the democratic world who already have the power to repeal ordinary laws, and in some cases constitutional provisions as well, by simple majority vote at any time have exercised such restraint even though no strong formal institutional barriers stand in the way of their repeal of these laws.[16] It is plausible to maintain that the strong informal institutional barriers that stand in the way of frequent and destabilizing repeal of laws by majority vote would also come to stand in the way of allowing laws to lapse so dramatically as to destabilize the country.[17] In the presence of such institutional barriers, the effect of a practice of periodic re-enactment, when measured in terms of the number of laws that are struck from the books, might differ little from the status quo.

If there would be such a bias in favour of the status quo, then a practice of Jeffersonian re-enactment might seem to be vulnerable to the opposite objection that it would do too little rather than too much. Why bother to introduce such a practice of re-enactment if it would make no difference to what is inscribed on the books and hence to the laws by which ordinary citizens are governed in their daily lives?[18] Wouldn't this process amount to little more than an empty ritual—a mere rubber stamp of renewal of the laws? A Jeffersonian could, I think, offer the following response to this challenge. Even if it would make no difference to what is written down on the statute books and hence to the policies that affect people in their daily lives, a require-

---

[16] Note that in present-day Britain it is arguably easier, institutionally speaking, to repeal a law than in the United States, since Britain's second legislative chamber has the power only to delay such repeal and its chief executive does not have an exercisable power to veto, whereas in the United States the two legislative chambers have equal say and the chief executive exercises a real power of veto. Yet Britain is no nearer the brink of anarchy than the United States.

[17] It is also worth noting that, in representative democracies as opposed to monarchies or dictatorships, those who govern must relinquish power unless they achieve reinstatement at the voting booth at fairly regular intervals. If Madison's argument against periodic re-enactment of laws is sound, why does it not also tell against periodic renewal of the terms of office of those who govern?

[18] One might ask a similar question about odious criminal laws that remain on the books though they are no longer enforced. (Sodomy laws in the United States, for example.) Why bother to strike these laws from the books if they make no difference to what people can do because they are not enforced? The answer here is that it is an evil in itself for the state formally to condemn such things as crimes.

ment of periodic re-enactment would nevertheless make a profound difference: it would formally render such laws the result of acts of the will of the living rather than the passively received legacy of the dead.[19] It would amount to an explicit, official recognition of the way things ought to be: a political society of equals in which the living govern themselves rather than one in which they are governed by outside forces.

2. *A collectivist proposal.* Some might try to distinguish the authority of deceased Americans in my example from the authority of the present-day British over living Americans by proposing a collectivist solution to the problem of intergenerational sovereignty which draws its inspiration from Hegel. The solution I have in mind posits the existence of a collective agent, the American people or society, that maintains its identity down through the ages and can bind itself far into the future even though all of the human beings that jointly constitute this entity at one point in time will be replaced over the years.[20] Perhaps the American people or society survives the demise of a majority of the human beings that constitute it at any one point in time just as a single human being survives the loss of the majority of the molecules in the body that constitute it at any given point in time.

Why, an advocate of the collectivist solution might ask the Jeffersonian, do you not recognize the existence of such an intergenerational temporal dimension to political society given that you recognize that a legitimate political society can span impressively large spatial distances?[21] Or, to put the point a bit less abstractly and more precisely, given that you already recognize that people in Alaska can

[19] Even the replacement of an existing set of rituals of state by another would have a salutary effect. This would be most pronounced in Britain, where the vestiges of hierarchy and subordination by accident of birth are placed on full display at the opening of each session of Parliament. The formal recognition on that day of a hierarchy of the monarch, her servants (i.e. her ministers), and her subjects, and of lords (some of whom are still hereditary) and commoners would be swept away and replaced by another set of rituals that formally recognizes the sovereignty of the people who inhabit the country at the time.

[20] Stephen Holmes notes that thinkers as diverse as Seneca, Aquinas, Bodin, Hobbes, and Rousseau have denied the power of an individual to bind himself in the future except by means of a promise to somebody other than himself (see Holmes, 'Precommitment and the Paradox of Democracy', in his *Passions and Constraint* (Chicago, Ill.: University of Chicago, 1995), 146–8). Their denials might cast doubt on the power of an individual to bind himself to himself irrevocably, but they do not cast doubt on the much more modest power of an individual to make a revocable decision which stands until that point at which he changes his mind. The collective agent requires only this more modest power in order to bind itself by majority vote of its constituents at one point in time for as long as it does not 'change its mind' by majority vote of its constituents at some subsequent point in time.

[21] Cf. Jeremy Waldron, *Law and Disagreement* (Oxford: Oxford University Press, 1999), 273.

have a legitimate say, through the legislators they send to Congress, over the federal laws that will govern people thousands of miles away in Florida, why are you so resistant to the recognition of the authority of the dead who are separated by years rather than miles from the living?

To this challenge I have two responses.

(*a*) First, if the powers of Alaskans over Floridians were strictly analogous to the powers of the dead over the living, then Alaskans would have the power singlehandedly to bind Floridians and not vice versa. Alaskans would have the power, by majority vote of Alaskans alone, to impose laws on Floridians which would bind them unless they repealed them, just as the Americans of one hundred years ago had the power, by majority vote, to impose laws on present-day Americans which bind them in the absence of their repeal. But Floridians would not have the power legally to bind Alaskans, just as the living do not have power to enact laws which apply retroactively to the dead. But nobody claims that the geographically defined parts of legitimate democratic communities have such singlehanded and asymmetric powers over other parts. Such geographic arrangements would be a throwback to the abuses of colonialism.

A defender of the rule of the dead over the living might respond that the aforementioned asymmetry in temporal power-relations is disanalogous to the asymmetry of colonial relations for the following reason. The temporal asymmetry is a natural and inoffensive consequence of the fact that it is impossible to know, and hence to follow, laws enacted by future generations, whereas this is not true of laws enacted by previous generations. Any geographic asymmetry in power relations would, by contrast, be imposed by human choice. In reply, I note that even if the impossibility of knowing future enactments were hypothesized away, we would not regard the laws of future generations as binding on the present generation. For suppose, *per impossibile*, that an oracle was known infallibly to disclose the laws which would be enacted in a given political society one hundred years hence.[22] It would be absurd to conclude that these laws had any morally binding force on the present generation now that they could be known and followed. Why, in the light of this fact, should laws enacted one hundred years ago have any morally binding force on the present generation?

---

[22] I am indebted to G. A. Cohen both for this example and for the lessons drawn from it in the following two sentences.

(*b*) My second response to the collectivist's challenge is that there is, in Lockean theory, a valid explanation of how geographically immense and legitimate political communities of members of the same generation can form, through the banding together of large numbers of contemporaries and the placing, by means of voluntary consensual transfer of their natural property rights, of the land which they own under common governance.[23] But there is no comparable valid explanation of how members of one generation can come to have authority over members of subsequent generations. A group of adults have the right collectively to bind themselves to a political authority, but no right to bind their descendants.

Now this is not to deny the existence of such a thing as the American people or society that persists across generations. Rather, it is to resist an appeal to such a persisting entity as a means of establishing the legitimacy of the laws of the dead. There may not be anything metaphysically suspect about the existence of such a persisting entity. But it is politically reactionary and unsound to invoke its authority over the living human beings that constitute it.[24]

3. *Tacit consent via non-repeal.* In his response to Jefferson's letter to him Madison makes an appeal to 'the received doctrine that a *tacit* assent may be given to established governments and laws, and that this assent is to be inferred from the omission of an express revocation'.[25] Might such a doctrine of tacit consent provide a solution to the problem of intergenerational sovereignty? Does the mere 'omission of an express revocation' by the members of a given society genuinely constitute morally binding tacit consent to the laws which others seek to impose upon the members of that society?[26] It does not. For consider,

---

[23] See Ch. 5 above.

[24] It would also be politically reactionary and unsound to invoke a duty of ancestral piety in order to justify the sovereignty of the dead over the living. Even if we were to grant such a duty of great-great-great-great-grandfatherly piety, and to grant that it grounds an obligation to obey ancestral laws, this duty would not fully bind the great majority of Americans to the laws of the United States who cannot trace their lineage back to those who resided in the thirteen confederated former colonies at the time of the establishment of the United States. It does little better to appeal to the fact that, whether or not they are the ancestors of present-day Americans, previous generations of Americans have profoundly affected the cultural identities of present-day Americans. For, this fact, while undoubtedly true, does not carry with it any obligation to obey these transmitters of culture. For if it did, then those young adults around the world who have, in recent years, been profoundly influenced by American sitcoms, movies, fast-food franchises, and marketers of clothing and footwear would, at least in some small measure, thereby be bound to obey the decrees of present-day Americans (or their corporate bosses).

[25] Madison, Letter to Jefferson, 440n.

[26] As shall become clear in the final section of this chapter, such Madisonian tacit consent by means of silence differs in significant respects from the ideal of free and equal Lockean tacit consent by means of residence that I endorse.

once again, the case with which I began this chapter—that in which Britain proclaims that its law apply not just to Britain, but also to the United States. In that case, the mere 'omission of an express revocation' of these laws by the American Congress clearly does not constitute morally binding consent to these laws. Why, then—once again to press the question which constitutes the problem of intergenerational sovereignty—should the 'omission of an express revocation' of the laws made by the American Congress several decades ago constitute morally binding consent by the living to these legislative enactments of the dead?[27]

One answer to this question points to a difference in the beliefs and consequent practices of Americans regarding the legitimacy of the laws of the dead versus the laws of a foreign country. The laws of the dead are nearly universally believed by Americans to be legitimate when applied to the living, and the practices of American judges, legislators, and law-enforcement officers as well as the public at large reflect this belief, as does the official record of what is taken to be the law of the land. Indeed, these beliefs, practices, and records may be sufficient to make it the case that these laws of the dead are among the laws of the living (though whether they *legitimately* govern the living is a further question). By contrast, the laws of Britain in our thought-experiment would, if Britain were to attempt to apply them to the United States, no doubt be nearly universally regarded by Americans as illegitimate in their application to them. So perhaps we should say that 'omission of an express revocation' of laws constitutes tacit consent to these laws if, furthermore, there is widespread belief in the legitimacy of these laws and this belief is reflected in the record books and the practices of government officials and the public at large.

At this point, one who believes that intergenerational sovereignty is a genuine problem is likely to protest that it is precisely the justifiability of a belief in the legitimacy of the laws of the dead which is at issue. Does it not beg the question to appeal to such beliefs in solving the problem of intergenerational sovereignty? Not necessarily. This is

---

[27] If the logic of Jefferson's argument did not apply to the United States Constitution, then it might have been possible to differentiate the laws handed down from the past from the laws of a foreign country in the following way. Unlike the laws of a foreign country, these laws of the past, though enacted as the result of the votes of legislators who are now dead, were formally acts of an institution—namely, the American Congress—which persists to this day and maintains its legitimate authority over Americans across time by virtue of the persisting legitimacy of the Constitution which legitimizes this institution. But since, by the logic of the Jeffersonian argument, the Constitution itself must lapse unless it is re-enacted as frequently as statutes, the legitimacy of the Congress lapsed long ago given the absence of any Jeffersonian re-enactment of the Constitution over the years.

because the presence or absence of such a belief might be morally relevant even if we have not yet settled the question of whether that belief is justified. The belief, even if not (yet) justified, that these laws are legitimate might provide grounds for concluding that the living have tacitly consented to, by refraining from repealing, these laws and therefore that these laws legitimately govern them. This belief would be rendered true by virtue of such tacit consent, but it would not stand in need of any independent justification on the theory of tacit consent now under consideration.

Although it may not beg the question, this theory of tacit consent nevertheless faces other difficulties. One problem is that it does not explain why the laws of the dead legitimately govern those dissenters who believe that these laws are illegitimate, where, for example, they believe this because they believe that the dead have no more right to govern the living of a given society than do the living of another society. Whether or not they are justified in believing this, one cannot infer tacit consent in their case simply on the basis of their 'omission of an express revocation of the laws'. Indeed, we cannot even make sense of the claim that any individual, in a democracy, ever omits to expressly revoke a law. This is because of the fact that, in a democracy, the power expressly to revoke a law resides in the majority of the living rather than in any individual. So the consent in question to which Madison appeals must be the tacit consent of the majority of the living rather than the consent of any or each individual.

Even if we allow that the consent of the majority of the living might bind dissenting individuals, we are still faced with a second problem. The theory of tacit consent under consideration leaves open the following possibility: that, in the absence of repeal, the laws of the past would be rendered legitimate over the living if they are thought so by enough people even if this thought is manifestly unjustified. Absurdities abound in this possibility. To illustrate one such absurdity, let us suppose that archaeologists unearth the remains of a long-lost civilization on American soil, including a detailed legal code decipherably etched on stone tablets. Suppose that these tablets declare that these laws and no others shall apply to all henceforth who reside on this soil unless and until that point in time at which these very laws are explicitly repealed by majority vote of the living.

Imagine that contemporary Americans come to think that the laws etched on these tablets constitute the law of the land to this day. As a consequence of these thoughts, they begin to behave in all manner of ways as if they are legitimately governed by these ancient laws. It would follow from the theory of tacit consent under discussion that these thoughts and the consequent behaviour would, in conjunction with the failure to repeal these laws, render these ancient laws the legitimate law of the land today. But of course no such thing follows from such deluded thoughts.

I submit that the unrepealed laws of the Constitution of the United States enshrined under glass in the National Archives in Washington, DC—and the Congressional statutes to which this Constitution gave rise long ago—are rendered no more legitimate by virtue of the fact that Americans think that, and consequently behave as if, these laws legitimately govern them. If what I have said in the previous section is right, there is, for example, no sound collectivist or communitarian argument which would serve to distinguish the soundness of these thoughts about this document under glass from the thoughts about the imagined tablets etched in stone.

Conclusion: Lockean consent. I hope, by now, to have provided good grounds for a preference for the Jeffersonian proposal over the status quo.[28] I believe that any actually existing democracy which adopted this proposal would more fully realize the ideals of democracy and the popular sovereignty of the living over the living. I would like, however, to close by drawing attention to a problem with Jefferson's proposal.[29] In the light of this problem we will see that Jefferson's policy would not fully realize these ideals even if it would realize them more fully than any actually existing democracy does. Finally, I will point the way to a Lockean solution to this problem which would fully realize these ideals.

---

[28] I have not, of course, dealt with each and every objection to Jefferson's proposal. Alon Harel, for example, has suggested that the Jeffersonian proposal is superfluous because the Supreme Court has already updated and legitimized the Bill of Rights by interpreting its content in the light of contemporary circumstances through a variety of decisions over the years. Such interpretations have served, time and again, to renew the twenty-year lease of the original document. There are, I think, three problems with this claim. (*a*) In actual fact, it is only in the past century or so that the Supreme Court has made its voice heard to any significant degree regarding the content of the Bill of Rights, which was well past the point that the original lease on the Bill of Rights had lapsed. (*b*) More significantly, even if the Supreme Court had, via interpretation, updated each of the provisions of the Bill of Rights at regular intervals of less than twenty years over the past two centuries, it is hardly a response to the objection that the Bill of Rights lacks *democratic* legitimacy to point to the fact that it has regularly been brought into line with contemporary norms by various majorities of unelected judges with lifetime tenure. (*c*) Finally, Jefferson's argument can be applied to the decisions of the Supreme Court itself. Why, in the absence of positive reaffirmation by living justices at regular intervals, should the dead hand of past Supreme Court decisions be allowed to hold sway?

[29] Cf. Madison's letter in response, in which he offers a challenge to Jefferson which is, in certain respects, similar to the one that I am about to offer.

The problem reveals itself once we try to answer the following question: What sort of obligation to obey the law, if any, would the young have who have reached the age of majority but not yet had a chance to vote (either directly or through their representatives) for or against the re-enactment of the laws? A very small minority will be fortunate enough to reach the age of majority on precisely the date of such a vote on re-enactment. But the vast majority will have to wait, in some cases for as long as twenty years, before they have a chance to vote on the re-enactment of the laws which govern them. Presumably Jefferson would have to say that those who have not yet had the opportunity to vote on re-enactment have no obligation whatsoever to obey the Constitution and other laws.[30] But this would be an unsettling consequence of his theory. Admittedly, even if it had this consequence, the young would still be bound by the 'moral law' to refrain from doing those things which, in addition to being illegal, are immoral and would be immoral even if they were not illegal. But the young would not have any moral obligation to refrain from doing those or any other things *because they are illegal.*

Could Jefferson find a way, without undermining his case for the expiration of the laws, to bring the young under the authority of the laws of the dead and hence to close this potentially twenty-year window of anarchy that the young would otherwise enjoy? I do not see how he could. Either the ground of the obligation of the young would be based upon their consent upon reaching the age of majority, or it would not.

Suppose, on the one hand, that the young would be obliged to obey these laws on some grounds other than their own consent. If Jefferson allows that the young can be bound without their consent by a group of people other than themselves, then how can he maintain his protest against the binding of all of the living of a nation by the dead or by a foreign nation? Why are the old and the middle-aged not also bound in the manner of the young? Why, in other words, would those non-consensual grounds that bind the young not be sufficient to bind all of the living to laws passed by those who are now dead?

Suppose, on the other hand, that the obligation of the young to obey these laws is grounded in their consent. In this case, the consent to the

---

[30] Might the young at least be bound by those laws which were newly enacted after they reached the age of majority? Even here there is some doubt, since presumably these laws gain their legitimacy by virtue of the fact that they were enacted by institutions and procedures which themselves are legitimized by the Constitution. But it is not clear that the young can be so bound by the Constitution, given that they have not had the opportunity to vote for or against that Constitution.

laws of the dead by the young upon reaching the age of majority would render Jefferson's proposal superfluous as there would be no further need for periodic Jeffersonian renewal of the laws.

I shall now explain how the obligation of the young could plausibly be grounded in their consent and how such consent would render Jefferson's proposal superfluous. A genuinely satisfying account of the conditions under which the laws of the dead would legitimately bind the living can be found in a theory of tacit consent which we have not yet considered. This theory is a modified version of Locke's theory of consent. Before presenting the theory itself, I shall briefly sketch Locke's own theory from which it derives.

Locke writes that '*a child is born a subject of no country or government*. He is under his father's tuition and authority, till he comes to age of discretion [on his twenty-first birthday]; and then he is a freeman, at liberty what government he will put himself under, what body political he will unite himself to' (II. 118). On this point, Jefferson is at one with Locke. But, unlike Jefferson, Locke also believes that the dead could legitimately exert their influence on the living in the following way. He believes that the first generation to confront an expanse of unowned land had the rights to acquire ownership over, and to place under the governance of their laws, this land in perpetuity. Hence, even though members of succeeding generations are technically 'freemen' upon reaching the age of majority, they could come to be bound, by virtue of their tacit consent, to obey the laws of their ancestors by inheriting, or even by setting foot on, the land of their ancestors. They would be bound for as long as they owned or set foot upon this land, in much the same way that an individual is bound to obey the laws of somebody's household by setting foot in that household.[31]

To illustrate how the problem of intergenerational sovereignty would be solved if people were so bound to obey, let us suppose that a new society is created and its laws enacted by a group of adult settlers upon a newly discovered island. According to Jefferson, the laws of this society ought in the absence of renewal to lapse when the generation which founded this society has passed from the scene. As a means of honouring this principle, let us stipulate, as was proposed above, that the laws are to lapse in twenty years in the absence of renewal. What is the status of the young who have attained the age of majority after the enactment of the laws, are now beyond the age of majority, but who have not yet had a chance to vote on the re-

---

[31] See Ch. 5 Sect. II above for a fuller account of Lockean tacit consent.

enactment of the laws because their twenty-year lease has not yet expired? If they have tacitly consented, in a fashion that morally binds them, to the laws upon reaching the age of majority simply by remaining within the boundaries of the country that governs them, then their consent would be sufficient to sustain the life of the laws beyond the term of twenty years. This is because the morally binding consent of the young upon reaching the age of majority would be sufficient to ensure that society would never reach a point at which a majority of living adults have neither voted for or against the enactment of the laws (either directly or through their representatives) nor consented to be bound by these laws after their enactment. Hence, society would never reach a point at which the living are governed by the dead hand of the past, since the consent of the young would continually breathe new life into these laws.

If, therefore, we are entitled to the supposition that those who attain the age of majority offer their morally binding tacit consent via residence to the laws that govern them, then we will have solved the problem of intergenerational sovereignty.

For reasons familiar and not so familiar, we are not entitled to this supposition at present. The familiar reason has to do with the unfreedom of such consent. The less familiar reason has to do with the unsoundness of Locke's claim that the first generation to confront an expanse of unowned land had the rights to acquire ownership over all this land, and to place this land under the governance of their laws, in perpetuity.[32] If they lack such rights, then it is hard to see how an alleged tacit consent by residence would be any more effective a means of placing the living under the authority of the dead than it would be as a means of placing the members of one country under the authority of another. It is, moreover, manifestly clear that Americans would not offer their morally binding tacit consent to the laws passed by Britain in our example above simply by continuing to remain on American soil.

I have argued in Chapter 5 that in order to ensure that tacit consent by residence is morally binding some fairly radical steps involving the egalitarian redistribution of worldly resources and the decentralization and pluralizing of political societies must be taken to ensure that such consent is freely given in circumstances of genuine equality. In the light of the fact that Jefferson's own solution to the problem of intergenerational sovereignty cannot cover those who have just

---

[32] See Ch. 5 Sect. II above, where, like Jefferson, I reject the Lockean view that our ancestors possessed the authority to bind those who set foot on their land after their deaths (see Jefferson, Letter to Madison, 959–60, 963).

reached the age of majority—and opens up a potentially twenty-year window of anarchy—we can now see that we have good reason to move beyond the Jeffersonian proposal and toward the realization of these conditions of equality and plurality under which mere residence within the borders of society would constitute freely given, genuinely morally binding consent. The need to solve the problem of intergenerational sovereignty provides further grounds to realize the Lockean left-libertarian ideal of political society as a voluntary association.

BIBLIOGRAPHY

Anderson, Robert, and DeTurk, Peter, 'United States Life Tables, 1999', *National Vital Statistics Report*, 50/6 (Hyattsville, Md.: National Center for Health Statistics, 21 March 2002).

Anscombe, Elizabeth, *The Collected Philosophical Papers of G. E. M. Anscombe*, iii. *Ethics, Religion, and Politics* (Minneapolis, Minn.: University of Minnesota Press, 1981).

Arneson, Richard, 'Equality and Equality of Opportunity for Welfare', *Philosophical Studies*, 56 (1989): 77–93.

——'Liberalism, Distributive Subjectivism, and Equal Opportunity for Welfare', *Philosophy and Public Affairs*, 19 (1990): 158–94.

——'Primary Goods Reconsidered', *Noûs*, 24 (1990): 429–54.

Barry, Brian, *Justice as Impartiality* (Oxford: Oxford University Press, 1995).

——'You Have to Be Crazy to Believe It', *TLS* 25 Oct. 1996, 28.

Beitz, Charles, 'Tacit Consent and Property Rights', *Political Theory*, 8 (1980): 487–502.

Christiano, Thomas, *The Rule of the Many: Fundamental Issues in Democratic Theory* (Boulder, Colo.: Westview Press, 1996).

Christman, John, 'Self-Ownership, Equality, and the Structure of Property Rights', *Political Theory*, 19 (1991): 28–46.

Cohen, G. A., 'Self-Ownership, World-Ownership, and Equality', in Frank Lucash (ed.), *Justice and Equality Here and Now* (Ithaca, NY: Cornell University Press, 1986).

——'Self-Ownership, World-Ownership, and Equality: Part II', *Social Philosophy and Policy*, 3 (1986): 77–96.

——'On the Currency of Egalitarian Justice', *Ethics*, 99 (1989): 906–44.

——'Incentives, Inequality, and Community', in Grethe B. Peterson (ed.), *The Tanner Lectures on Human Values*, xiii (Salt Lake City, Utah: University of Utah Press, 1992).

——'The Pareto Argument for Inequality', *Social Philosophy and Policy*, 12 (1995): 160–85.

——*Self-Ownership, Freedom, and Equality* (Cambridge: Cambridge University Press, 1995).

——Letter, *TLS* 8 Nov. 1996, 19.

——'Expensive Taste Rides Again', unpublished.

Dahl, Robert, *Democracy and its Critics* (New Haven, Conn.: Yale University Press, 1989).

Davis, Nancy, 'Abortion and Self-Defense', *Philosophy and Public Affairs*, 13 (1984): 175–207.

Dworkin, Ronald, 'Do Liberty and Equality Conflict?', in Paul Barker (ed.), *Living as Equals* (Oxford: Oxford University Press, 1996).

——*Sovereign Virtue* (Cambridge, Mass.: Harvard University Press, 2000).

Feinberg, Joel, 'The Expressive Function of Punishment', *Monist*, 49 (1965): 397–423.

Foot, Philippa, *Virtues and Vices* (Berkeley, Calif.: University of California Press, 1978).

——'Killing and Letting Die', in Jay Garfield and Patricia Hennessey (eds.), *Abortion: Moral and Legal Perspectives* (Amherst, Mass.: University of Massachusetts Press, 1984).

——'Morality, Action, and Outcome', in Ted Honderich (ed.), *Morality and Objectivity* (London: Routledge and Kegan Paul, 1985).

Freeman, Samuel, 'Illiberal Libertarians: Why Libertarianism Is Not a Liberal View', *Philosophy and Public Affairs*, 30 (2001): 105–51.

Gauthier, David, *Morals by Agreement* (Oxford: Oxford University Press, 1986).

Gellner, Ernest, *Nations and Nationalism* (Oxford: Blackwell, 1983).

Hart, H. L. A., *Punishment and Responsibility* (Oxford: Oxford University Press, 1967).

Hartley, L. P., *The Go-Between* (New York: New York Review of Books, 2002).

Holmes, Stephen, *Passions and Constraint* (Chicago, Ill.: University of Chicago, 1995).

Hume, David, *Essays: Moral, Political, and Literary*, ed. T. H. Green and T. H. Grose (London: Longmans, 1882).

——*A Treatise of Human Nature*, ed. David Norton and Mary Norton (Oxford: Oxford University Press, 2000).

Jakes, Dale, and Jakes, Connie, *False Prophets: The Firsthand Account of a Husband–Wife Team Working for the FBI and Living in Deepest Cover with the Montana Freemen* (Los Angeles, Calif.: NewStar Media, 1998).

Jefferson, Thomas, *Thomas Jefferson: Writings*, ed. Merrill D. Peterson (New York: Library of America, 1984).

Kamm, Frances, *Creation and Abortion* (New York: Oxford University Press, 1992).

——*Morality, Mortality*, 2 vols. (New York: Oxford University Press, 1993, 1996).

Klosko, George, *The Principle of Fairness and Political Obligation* (Lanham: Rowman & Littlefield, 1992).

Kukathas, Chandran, 'Are There Any Cultural Rights?' *Political Theory*, 20 (1992): 105–39.

Lijphart, Arend, 'Self-Determination versus Pre-Determination of Ethnic Minorities in Power-Sharing Systems', in Will Kymlicka (ed.), *The Rights of Minority Cultures* (Oxford: Oxford University Press, 1995).

Lloyd Thomas, David, *Locke on Government* (London: Routledge, 1995).

Locke, John, *An Essay concerning Human Understanding*, ed. Peter Nidditch (Oxford: Oxford University Press, 1975).

——*A Letter concerning Toleration* (Indianapolis, Ind.: Hackett, 1983).

——*Two Treatises of Government*, ed. Peter Laslett (Cambridge: Cambridge University Press, 1988).

Madison, James, *The Writings of James Madison*, ed. Gaillard Hunt, 9 vols. (New York: G. P. Putnam's Sons, 1904).

Mill, John Stuart, *On Liberty* (Indianapolis, Ind.: Hackett, 1978).

Nagel, Thomas, *Equality and Partiality* (New York: Oxford University Press, 1991).

Nozick, Robert, *Anarchy, State, and Utopia* (New York: Basic Books, 1974).

——*Philosophical Explanations* (Cambridge, Mass.: Harvard University Press, 1981).

Otsuka, Michael, 'Killing the Innocent in Self-Defense', *Philosophy and Public Affairs*, 23 (1994): 74–94.

——'Quinn on Punishment and Using Persons as Means', *Law and Philosophy*, 15 (1996): 201–8.

——'Kamm on the Morality of Killing', *Ethics*, 108 (1997): 197–207.

——'Self-Ownership and Equality: A Lockean Reconciliation', *Philosophy and Public Affairs*, 27 (1998): 65–92.

——'Making the Unjust Provide for the Least Well Off', *Journal of Ethics*, 2 (1998): 247–59.

Quinn, Warren, 'The Right to Threaten and the Right to Punish', *Philosophy and Public Affairs*, 14 (1985): 327–73.

——'Actions, Intentions, and Consequences: The Doctrine of Double Effect', *Philosophy and Public Affairs*, 18 (1989): 334–51.

——*Morality and Action* (Cambridge: Cambridge University Press, 1993).

Rawls, John, *A Theory of Justice* (Cambridge, Mass.: Harvard University Press, 1971).

——*Political Liberalism* (New York: Columbia University Press, 1993).

——*Justice as Fairness: A Restatement* (Cambridge, Mass.: Harvard University Press, 2001).

Raz, Joseph, *The Morality of Freedom* (Oxford: Oxford University Press, 1986).

Roemer, John, *Theories of Distributive Justice* (Cambridge, Mass.: Harvard University Press, 1996).

Scanlon, T. M., 'The Moral Basis of Interpersonal Comparisons', in Jon Elster and John Roemer (eds.), *Interpersonal Comparisons of Well-Being* (Cambridge: Cambridge University Press, 1991).

——*What We Owe to Each Other* (Cambridge, Mass.: Harvard University Press, 1998).

Simmons, A. John, *The Lockean Theory of Rights* (Princeton, NJ: Princeton University Press, 1992).

——*On the Edge of Anarchy* (Princeton, NJ: Princeton University Press, 1993).

Simmons, A. John, 'Justification and Legitimacy', *Ethics*, 109 (1999): 739–71.
——'On the Territorial Rights of States', *Philosophical Issues*, 35 (2001) (supplement to *Noûs*): 300–26.
Sreenivasan, Gopal, *The Limits of Lockean Rights in Private Property* (New York: Oxford University Press, 1995).
Steiner, Hillel, 'The Natural Right to the Means of Production', *Philosophical Quarterly*, 27 (1977): 41–9.
——'Capitalism, Justice, and Equal Starts', *Social Philosophy and Policy*, 5 (1987): 49–71.
——*An Essay on Rights* (Oxford: Blackwell, 1994).
Thomson, Judith Jarvis, *Rights, Restitution, and Risk* (Cambridge, Mass.: Harvard University Press, 1986).
——'Self-Defense', *Philosophy and Public Affairs*, 20 (1991): 283–310.
US Supreme Court, *Wisconsin v. Yoder*, 406 US 205 (1972).
Vallentyne, Peter, and Steiner, Hillel (eds.), *Left-Libertarianism and its Critics: The Contemporary Debate* (Basingstoke: Palgrave, 2000).
Van Parijs, Philippe, *Real Freedom for All* (Oxford: Oxford University Press, 1995).
Waldron, Jeremy, 'Special Ties and Natural Duties', *Philosophy and Public Affairs*, 22 (1993): 3–30.
——*Law and Disagreement* (Oxford: Oxford University Press, 1999).
Wolff, Jonathan, *Robert Nozick* (Palo Alto, Calif.: Stanford University Press, 1991).

INDEX